Called by Name

Twelve Guideline Meditations for Diocesan Priests

Reverend Michael E. Giesler

Copyright © 2011 Michael Edward Giesler
All rights reserved.

ISBN: 1-4663-7123-4
ISBN-13: 9781466371231

TABLE OF CONTENTS

VOCATION 1

LIFE OF PRAYER. 7

SERVING THE FAITHFUL 17

HUMILITY 27

SUPERNATURAL HOPE AND OPTIMISM. 35

FIDELITY TO THE CHURCH. 43

HOLY MASS AND THE EUCHARIST 51

HOLY PURITY AND CELIBACY 59

SHARING CHRIST'S CHALLENGE OF HOLINESS. 69

REDEMPTIVE SACRIFICE 79

CARING FOR OUR BROTHERS IN THE PRIESTHOOD 85

MARY OUR MOTHER 93

FOREWORD

During the 2009-2010 Year of the Priest, Father Giesler composed twelve reflections on diocesan priesthood, inspired by the life and writings of Saints John Mary Vianney, Phillip Neri, and Josemaría Escrivá. He did this in addition to writing and seeing published a helpful *Guidebook for Confessors*. All twelve of these meditations, published here as *Called by Name*, have an appealing and practical style, interspersed with personal prayer; they address the life and challenges of diocesan priests as they begin the second decade of the 21st century.

In one of these first reflections Father Giesler affirms that the "very origin of priesthood was in the prayer of Christ at the Last Supper, as He gave his apostles the power to consecrate in His name, and prayed for their unity with Him and one another." The rest of the book is truly a development of this idea—covering such essential topics as redemptive sacrifice, service to the faithful, supernatural hope, commitment to celibacy, and devotion to Mary, Mother of priests.

The book incorporates many quotes from Holy Scripture, the *Catechism of the Catholic Church*, and the writings of Blessed Pope John Paul II. It specifically develops key guidelines from the Holy See's *Directory for the Life and Ministry of Priests* (1994). I was particularly moved by the chapter on priestly fraternity, which gives practical advice on helping our brother priests to persevere in their vocation, with hope and good humor.

In sum, *Called by Name* is ideal spiritual reading for the busy contemporary priest; it effectively focuses him on the purpose of his ordination, and provides him with specific ways to grow in holiness of life.

Most Reverend Robert J. Carlson
Archbishop of Saint Louis

INTRODUCTION

The purpose of this brief book is to offer diocesan priests some guideline reflections to help them to fulfill their great mission—to give glory to God in all that they do, and to serve the Church and her people with generosity. The tone is meant to be reflective and inspirational, with examples drawn from contemporary life, and with prayerful dialogue and personal aspirations interspersed at certain points in order to help the reader to pray also.

The reflections cover such topics as vocation, the work of the priest, life of prayer, humility, obedience to their Ordinary, love for celibacy, devotion to Mary, helping the poor through the works of mercy, having hope and giving hope to others, fraternity for other priests, and making Holy Mass to be the center of our priesthood. All of these topics of course overlap, so the reader should not be surprised if he finds certain key concepts and quotations repeated and emphasized in the different sections.

The first chapter after vocation is about our life of prayer, or intimacy with Christ. Without the desire to be with Christ, and to give glory to God, our priesthood could easily turn into activism. *Nemo dat quod non habet*, the proven scholastic adage had it: no one gives what he does not have. If we are to give people God's truth and love, we must experience it somehow in ourselves first, and yes hunger and yearn for it—even before preaching and administering the sacraments to others. For priesthood primarily is about deep personal commitment to, and love for God and His Son, and desire to give glory to God in all that we do. To this end Christ himself pledged that He would be with us always, to keep us faithful and to help us fulfill our commitment: "And lo, I am with you always, to the close of the age" (*Mt* 28:20).

Loving and generous service to our people will necessarily follow.

We have a large company of priests that have gone before us—holy men who gave their lives for the Church and others, and who truly put God and his glory above all other things. They are not only examples for us, but saints that we can invoke to intercede for us in all aspects of our ministry. To them, and particularly to Saints John Mary Vianney, Phillip Neri, and Josemaría Escrivá this book is dedicated.

Bibliographical Note

Besides the writings of priest saints and the most recent Popes and Magisterium, this book refers regularly to the *Directory for the Life and Ministry of Priests*, a document of the Congregation of the Clergy published in 1994. It was requested by the Synod of Bishops held in 1990, and also reflects many of the insights of Pope John Paul II's Post-Synodal Apostolic Exhortation *Pastores dabo vobis* (1992). For purposes of brevity, quotes from the Directory will simply be identified as DLM, together with the section number. The English edition was produced by the Libreria Editrice Vaticana in 1994.

All quotes from Holy Scripture are from Revised Standard Version Catholic Edition (RSVCE). Certain Scripture quotes, along with my personal prayers and reflections are put in *italics*.

VOCATION

Blessed be the God and Father of our Lord Jesus Christ, who has blessed us in Christ with every spiritual blessing in the heavenly places, even as He chose us in Him before the foundation of the world, that we should be holy and blameless before Him (Eph 1:3-4). God includes all human beings in His Providence, but in a particular way, He chooses those who will be His priests and ministers. For the priest must continue the saving work of God's Son on earth; he must give glory to God through his works and words; he must be the minister of God's grace to his people, and a sign of the world to come. We need to give special thanks for this marvelous gift of priesthood, and try to renew our commitment to it more each day.

Our vocation takes into account many factors: our family history, our schooling, our temperament, and all the events—even those that seemed inconsequential at the time—that led us to the call of priesthood. Whenever they occurred they were workings of God's grace in our lives—perhaps in dramatic ways, perhaps in slow almost imperceptible ways. As Pope Benedict XVI stated to young people in Australia in 2008: "Life is not governed by chance; it is not random. Your very existence has been willed by God, blessed and given a purpose! Life is not just a succession of events and experiences. It is a search for the true, the good, and the beautiful. It is to this end that we make our choices; it is for this that we exercise our freedom….." (*Papal Welcome at Sydney Airport,* July 17, 2008) Now it is up to each one of us to correspond to that gift, for the glory and love of God first of all, and then for the service of the souls that he has entrusted to us.

Without doubt, each of us can say that he has been *called by name*—not only at our ordination ceremony, not only by our ordaining bishop, but by the Lord Christ himself. Our life was changed the day we were ordained first as deacons then as priests. Not only did we pass juridically from the lay state to the clerical state within the Church, but our souls received an indelible character upon them, marking us ontologically as Christ's ministers, and configuring us to him. From this day forward our lives are not for ourselves, but we are dedicated to God primarily and for his glory.

This is the first and primary reason for our priesthood. Just as Christ continually adored the Father and gave Him homage through His work, miracles, and finally His passion and death—we His priests are to do the same. Our life of prayer, our saying of the Breviary, our care for the parish and its duties are all for the praise and glory of God. Our sacramental work forms part of the immense liturgy that is taking place world-wide which gives public homage to God and His Goodness. Through our common priesthood and ministerial priesthood we share in Christ's three roles or *munera*, all of which give praise to God and serve His people: to teach in His name, to shepherd souls to Him, to sanctify. By preaching we give glory to the One who is Truth Himself—when we speak convincingly of His law, His commandments, and His saving plan for all mankind. All that we do is intimately connected with the mystery of Christ the God-man: "In this unique identity with Christ, the priest must be conscious that his life is a mystery totally grafted onto the mystery of Christ and of the Church in a new and specific way and that this engages him totally in pastoral activity and rewards him" (*Directory for the Life and Ministry of Priests* [*DLM*], n.6).

***

Let's pray earnestly to the Holy Spirit that our work never become merely bureaucratic or functional; routine is the biggest enemy of true fervor. There is something in all of us that can get used to mystery. Even though our lives are surrounded by the mystery of God's grace—particularly in the sacraments and spiritual direction—-we can unfortunately become "used to it all." *Lord, may I realize that holiness cannot be stuffed or preserved like a moose head on our wall. Lord, may I not let the days and years go by simply out of inertia, with no clear goals to improve myself—with your grace of course! In some way I must desire to be a priest each day with a renewed fervor, being open to the graces that God will send me. In this way I will truly love and give glory to God in everything that I do.*

Saint Paul, speaking of the vocation of the first Christians, and of himself, once wrote: "But we have this treasure in earthen vessels…" (II Cor.4:7). Despite the high calling to holiness that priesthood entails, we all recognize our littleness and even wretchedness many times. Yes, we all have this beautiful calling and this immense treasure of grace in vessels of clay—clay that is often cheap, brittle, too soft or too hard. Part of the beauty of our vocation is precisely to recognize our unworthiness.

I am sure that is why the Church wants to us to prostrate ourselves completely on the ground as part of the rite of ordination. We are nothing but dust, yet God through the bishop has chosen us. The more honestly we recognize our weaknesses, the more God will do through us and for us. Yes, we see pride and vanity in ourselves—perhaps when we view priesthood for advancement or human praise in some form. Yes, we can see anger and pettiness coming through in us—in gossip about others, in feelings of being unappreciated or slighted. Yes, we see lust and the disordered desire for comfort or pleasures that can lead to grave sins. Yes, we see sadness and melancholy tempting us to turn in upon ourselves and to give up. *O Lord, when faced with my wretchedness, may I pray to you those magnificent words that you spoke to the Apostle:* "My grace is sufficient for you, for my power is made perfect in weakness" (II *Cor* 12:9). God knew whom He was choosing when He gave us our vocation, and with His grace He can turn even the biggest defeats into moments of victory.

***

The call to priesthood is first of all then a personal call to give praise to God through our work and prayer. It is also a personal call to become saints. It would be a waste of time and energy if we were to try to make others holy and neglect our own spiritual lives. A priest must be a man of God and have Jesus Christ as his model. This means that literally everything that we do, from our first thought in the morning to our last thought at night, should be for the glory of God. Holiness (Hebrew: Kadosh) in Sacred Scripture really means two things: distance from sin and closeness to God. The first meaning seems negative, but it really isn't. By fleeing from sin and its occasions we will draw closer to God; in rejecting the negative we definitely choose the positive. And as our years of dedication go by, it is closeness to God that should occupy us the most, for a priest is basically a man who is deeply in love. His whole life exists to be with the One he loves—"le Bon Dieu" in the favorite expression of Saint John Mary Vianney.

The final test of any vocation is perseverance. "I am the vine, you are the branches. He who abides in Me, and I in him, he it is that bears much fruit" (Jn 15:5). *Abide ! What a beautiful old English word! It signifies not only being in a place—but remaining there in a fixed and permanent way. May I always abide in you, Lord, as your faithful priest and minister.* We have all known priests who have left, often in very painful circumstances for themselves and those around them, and frequently with scandal to the Church. We must realize that the ultimate goal of our calling as priests is to be faithful *to the end*. Let's resolve, again with God's constant help, to die in the state of grace and in the state of priesthood.

Though there are ceremonies for the initial ground breaking of buildings and monuments, the keystone or final stone is the most important. The famous Gateway Arch in Saint Louis, constructed in 1965 along the banks of the Mississippi, took several years to design and build. It could not stand on its own until the last metallic segment was placed at the top of the Arch; now it does stand on its own, a beautiful monument to westward expansion for all to see. May God be able to place that final segment in our own life, which exists for His glory. In the words of Saint Josemaria Escrivá in his little book *The Way*, which has been an inspiration for millions (both priests and laymen): "And what is the secret of perseverance? Love. Fall in love and you will not leave Him" (*The Way*, n. 999).

Though she did not receive the Sacrament of Holy Orders, Mary is the mother of all priests, and she possesses the greatest priestly soul of any human person who ever lived or will live. Her whole life was dedicated to giving glory to God, and she did so in the most perfect and complete way. Her self-giving was complete, from the moment of the Annunciation to her self-oblation on Calvary with her Son. As mother of the Church and channel of all graces, she intervened in a personal way in our own priestly vocation. Perhaps it was a word from her, or a smile of hers in heaven, that won us the invitation and grace to be priests of her Son. And her motherly care continues for each of us throughout our life—both in good times, and less good. Let's go often to her as we pray about priesthood and its duties, realizing that of all human persons she was the one who fulfilled her vocation best. With her priestly soul she is the model of all priests: in the way she prays, offers sacrifice, makes atonement for sins, and redeems us in union with her Son.

Mary Most holy, Mother of all priests, we go to you as small boys desiring to learn from you. Teach us to be true to our calling, as you were. For we too exist for the glory of God the Father. We too must bring His beloved Son to this world. We too must be sources of unity and inspiration for His bride the Holy Catholic Church. Teach us therefore to say yes to each of God's graces and illuminations, as you did; to have a vibrant faith, hope, and charity that will inform each day of our lives until we are able at last to join you and your Son, together with the Father and the Holy Spirit. Forever and ever. Amen.

LIFE OF PRAYER

"The glory which thou hast given Me I have given to them that they may be one even as We are one" (*Jn* 17:22). Our Lord spoke those words at the Last Supper, to remind His followers forever about the real source of effectiveness. The priority of a priest's life is to be always united to the Master; therefore he puts the things of God first, and in union with God, he serves others.

The very origin of priesthood was in the prayer of Christ at the Last Supper, as He gave His apostles the power to consecrate in His name, and prayed for their unity with Him and one another. "Born of these prayers, and called to renew a Sacrifice inseparable from these, priests maintain their ministry with a spiritual life to which they give absolute pre-eminence, avoiding any neglect due to other activities" (*DLM*, n.38). By putting his spiritual life first a priest is not being an egotist, nor is he shirking his duties to others, but is precisely fulfilling his vocation in a way that can really serve them. Ultimately, a priest is a man *of orders* and *under* orders. His mission is to be conformed to Christ the High Priest, and to direct his whole life accordingly. When he was ordained, he received the mission to become a holy priest, and to bring a thousand souls with him—at least—into Eternal Glory.

He must therefore have certain priorities in his life, which means that he has to say yes to some things, and no to others. First he must say yes to his greatest privilege and duty as a priest: to celebrate the Holy Sacrifice of the Mass with attention and devotion. It is the center of the Church's life, and of his own life. We should therefore prepare for it well, by spending a little time in prayer before it begins—either with the Breviary or a period of meditation. Many pious priests over the centuries have also invoked their *ministerial Archangel* before saying Mass. Devotion to our guardian angel is of course a solid devotion for all Christian men and women, but for us priests to have a ministerial archangel guiding us is particularly comforting. He will help us to administer the sacraments with piety, and to concentrate well on the prayers of the Mass, as he delivers our petitions directly to the Throne of Glory. Above all, we should be especially mindful that while celebrating the Holy Eucharist we are truly *Christ the Head* of His people, who makes acts of adoration, petition, atonement, and thanksgiving to the Father through the love of the Holy Spirit. The devout saying of the Mass will have a truly transforming effect in our lives. "Through Him, and with Him, and in Him...." we extend Christ's presence throughout our day in what we could descriptively call a *twenty-four hour Mass*, to use an expression of Saint Josemaría Escrivá.

There are many causes of disorder in our lives and of disunity from our goal. Perhaps one of the biggest dangers for us is activism. It's very easy for a priest to be caught up in a continuous round of appointments, phone calls, travel, committee meetings, and parish projects—to the point of losing his bearings. He can exhaust himself in a thousand different ways, even in *good* things because he's a priest; but he can easily miss the most important thing: to be a man of prayer and true charity. For this reason he needs the virtue of order which above all fosters his life of prayer and his relationship with Jesus Christ. "Precisely in order to effectively carry out his pastoral ministry, the priest must enter into a special and profound rapport with Christ the Good Shepherd, who alone remains the principal protagonist in any pastoral action" (*DLM*, n.38).

***

To foster this life of prayer, there are a number of holy practices that we priests should try to incorporate in our life, again with a sense of order and priority. The first we have already mentioned: daily Eucharistic celebration, with adequate preparation and attention. Next is frequent use of the sacrament of Confession, both for obtaining forgiveness of sins, and the specific grace to improve. We don't need to wait until we commit a mortal sin before going to Confession; there is much evidence that frequent confession actually prevents grave sin, since it makes us examine our conscience regularly, be honest with ourselves and God, and receive a sacramental grace to be stronger. Weekly Confession is strongly recommended for priests who are sincerely striving to become holy.

The saying of the breviary, with all of its parts, is an obligation that we assumed the day we were ordained. It is our contribution to the public prayer of the Church for the glory of God…and the Church with all of her faithful is counting on us to say it. Since order is the virtue by which we give priority to God and others, we should pray the breviary with devotion each day….even if we have distractions and subjectively appear to be getting little benefit from it. The benefit of the Divine Office is enormous, since each of its parts gives a special glory to God—the Psalmody, hymns, readings, and intercessions. When possible, we are encouraged to sing or pray the breviary with our brother priests—at workshops, retreats, or any fitting occasion. We can be sure that this collective prayer, of several brothers together gathered in Christ's name, is especially pleasing to God.

Good spiritual direction, begun in the seminary and continued after ordination, assures consistent growth in our spiritual life. None of us are good guides for our own souls, since we tend to be either too hard or too easy on ourselves. It is also difficult to see our faults objectively. For this reason we need a master or guide who can give us a good particular *examen* (see below), who will correct us when needed, and point us in the right direction. We also need someone with whom we can share the burdens and frustrations of our life. In choosing a good director, let's look particularly for three things: holiness of life, faithfulness to the Church's teachings, and experience in directing souls to Christ.

Related to good spiritual direction is the practice of daily examination of conscience. One of the best times to do this is at Night Prayer, if we are not too tired.

A good examination consists of looking at our day, and how we have done our duties and lived the virtues of a dedicated priest. First, of course, we should make note of any sins we have committed, whether mortal or venial, and try to make an act of perfect contrition for them, with the resolve to confess them as soon as possible. At the same time we may note many faults and imperfections, such as lack of attention in prayer, wasting time, thoughtless comments, or a complaining spirit or tone of voice. Again we can ask forgiveness for these lapses, and the grace to do better the next day. It may even be helpful to write down some of these resolutions in our notebook or palm recorder, so that we can review them the next day. Related to the spirit of examination is to have a good *particular examen*, that is, some specific point or effort to improve in a certain area, about which we have prayed, and have received advice from our spiritual director. Such a particular examen, for instance, could be focused on good use to time, living better custody of the eyes in matters of chastity, practicing temperance in food and drink, having a more positive tone of speech with those around us. The main point behind daily examination of conscience is that we not become lukewarm or complacent about our spiritual life; though sanctity is mostly God's work, we must also do our part by struggling sincerely against our own sins and failures.

***

"The prayer of a Christians is never a monologue," writes Saint Josemaría in his little book *The Way* (n.114). As priests we need to speak with Christ and his Mother in our own words each day. Mental prayer is different from vocal prayer, which usually involves fixed words or phrases such as the Father and Hail Mary. It is to speak with Christ in our own words, in a personal and spontaneous way, as we would speak with a good friend. And who could be a better friend than He? In talking with Christ about our work, our concerns, even our temptations, He can make us stronger, and console us. He can also provide us with good resolutions, affections, and inspirations that can carry us through the day and help us to be happier, more effective priests. If at times the words don't come to you in your prayer, you might simply want to sit before the tabernacle and let Him love you, as you try to love Him. This is a most beautiful prayer that also pleases God and can give great peace. At other times you may wish to take a book or the *lectio divina* of the day, and try to take some resolution or insight from it. The main thing is to establish a time each day for this indispensable personal time with God—at least 15 minutes—so that your life can be more focused, so that you can do everything through Him, with Him, in Him. Consistent mental prayer gives great peace to the soul, along with a special insight and energy necessary for our pastoral work.

The *Catechism of the Catholic Church* has three interesting sections titled *Prayer as Covenant*. "Christian prayer is a covenant relationship between God and man in Christ. It is the action of God and man, springing forth from both the Holy Spirit and ourselves, wholly directed to the Father, in union with the human will of the Son of God made man" (*CCC*, n.2564). As priests we are already involved in a personal covenant relationship with the Trinity and the Church, and prayer is the principal support of that covenant. For this reason all of us priests must learn to meditate and consider often the great truths of faith that are found in Sacred Scripture and the Traditions of the Church. Let's try to enter into the Gospel scenes each day and reflect on what they reveal to us: the divine power of Christ who cures and does miracles, the wonder of Nicodemus upon hearing that he must be born again, the sorrow of Peter at his denials. We also need to meditate often on magisterial documents concerning faith and morals, especially the writings of the Pope. But we should not pray only about contemporary issues, but also about the great perennial teachings of the Church on the Incarnation, Faith, Justification and the Sacraments. In this way our minds will truly be the mind of the Church herself, and we can give glory to God for his truth, as well as provide clear and true instruction for our people.

With meditation, we should also try to pray from the heart. Mere consideration of truth cannot be enough for us; somehow that truth must become interiorized in us. When we pray, we must therefore try to have personal contact with Christ and His Father, through the inspiration and love of the Holy Spirit. Let's ask the Spirit that our prayer be truly alive and effective, and not be done out of routine, or mere external fulfillment. The more we advance in prayer, the more interior it will become. It will truly come from the heart. "The heart is the dwelling place where I am, where I live; according to the Semitic or Biblical expression, the heart is the place 'to which I withdraw'.....The heart is the place of decision, deeper than our psychic drives. It is the place of truth, where we choose life or death. It is the place of encounter, because as image of God we live in relation; it is the place of covenant" (*CCC*, n.2563). As we can see prayer from the heart is far more than emotions or affections, though they have their place. Prayer from the heart involves the whole man, so to speak. It involves our interior attitudes and convictions, and daily decisions that we make. With good prayer these convictions, literally what motivates us and "makes us tick," will become fortified and directed to real holiness.

As a result of our covenant relationship with God, and our sincere conversation with Him each day, we will become more and more like Christ and even become *ipse Christus*—Christ Himself. We will learn to make resolutions that make us more like Him—in the way we deal with others, in the way we perform the liturgy and preach, in the voluntary sacrifices that we offer, in the way we live celibacy for the sake of God's Kingdom. We will little by little acquire the affections of Christ the man—His zeal for the things of God, His tender love for all people, His joy at seeing the truth proclaimed and the devil defeated, His sorrow at sin and spiritual blindness. We will receive inspirations, about not only the profound truths of our faith but also the little things that we can do better each day, and how to improve the relationships that we have with others. All of this comes from that complete engagement of mind and heart that prayer should be, which gradually transforms our lives into the life of Christ Himself.

In the modern world we are bombarded with discordant words and ideas. They come from television, the internet, news articles, and people's comments on the street. It is very easy for us to be confused or at least troubled by these things, despite years of seminary training. For our life of prayer, clarity of mind, and effective preaching, we need good spiritual reading every day. Preferably it will be from the works of great saints and theologians, that is, of those men and women who themselves have lived close to God and helped thousands more to do so, both in their own times and now. A good spiritual book, especially one recommended by your spiritual guide, will offer and re-offer you the great truths of revelation in a deep yet practical way: truths about sin and redemption, about the sacraments, about prayer, about current moral issues. At times the reading could be a series of meditations or books on the lives of the saints. The main point of good spiritual reading is that it should help you as a priest to know the things of God and draw closer to Him in your daily life.

Devotion to Mary is essential for Catholics and, in a special way, for priests. Though the final chapter of this little book is dedicated to her, it is worth speaking of her particularly in the context of prayer: *De Maria, numquam satis*, as the wise adage goes: about Mary, you can never say enough. Just as she has a personal love for us, because she sees the image of her Son in us, we must have a personal love for her. Since she is Mediatrix of all graces (a common teaching of the Church), we can have the moral certainty that she obtained the grace of vocation for each one of us. *Mary, thank you for remembering me and favoring me…thank you for your help in all the difficult moments of my life, especially for living purity and perseverance.* As good sons, we must be desirous to be with her, to speak with her—either by short aspirations each day, or by longer devotions such as the Rosary.

By saying the complete Rosary each day, or at least one of the four parts, we enter more directly into the lives of Mary and her Son. In a mysterious way their joys, inspirations, sorrows, and triumphs become ours. Let's find the moments each day, no matter how busy we are, to spend time with our Mother. In the words of Father Suarez in his classic book *About Being a Priest*: "Of all the devotions we can have, the most lovable and perhaps the most spontaneous and instinctive is our devotion to the Blessed Virgin. Our heart is made for love and she is the 'Mother of Fair Love', the most noble and purest love of all….. The priest especially can find no better counselor, no surer guide, no stronger support, no more self-sacrificing help. The Mother of Jesus, who is the eternal Priest, knows well how hard a priest's work is, she fully understands its dangers, its misunderstandings, its difficulties; she realizes better than anyone else how much heroism is involved in being a mediator. Therefore, she softens the harshness of his life, she brings sweetness to his sorrow and company to his solitude, she gives him strength to bear misunderstanding, support in times of trial and hope in the midst of the struggle" (Scepter Publishers, New York, 1996, page 213).

***

Monthly days of recollection supply a needed oasis for prayer and reflection in a priest's life. It could take the form of a quiet day in the country, where one can read, walk, and reflect...or an event organized by a group in the Church for this purpose, such as those offered by Opus Dei and other institutions that promote the sanctity of priests. A fruitful day of recollection will preferably include some time before the Blessed Sacrament, which is the center of our priesthood and the focal point of our devotion, one or two conferences on some aspect of the spiritual life, and an opportunity for Confession or spiritual direction. By going to these regularly, we can obtain valuable ideas from others that will enrich our faith and prayer life. Literally, they help us to "recollect" ourselves, and put as one all the different segments of our experiences each month, so that we can see our path more clearly and make some good resolutions. It is often a fine opportunity for priestly fraternity as well, since many recollections include time for a meal before or afterwards, when we can get to know our brother priests better, and exchange friendship and experiences with them.

The yearly retreat for priests, besides being mandated by Church law, is founded on ancient tradition and fills a great need in our life. Our soul, at least once a year, needs a more intense and personal time of prayer for a number of days. The retreat affords us the chance to look at our life more deeply and calmly, without the need to rush back to the rectory, make a phone call, or visit someone. With several days ahead of us that are free from external commitments, we can really go deeper with God in our minds and hearts....as Elijah did when he made his retreat on the mountain and heard God in the form of a still, small voice (see *I Kings* 19:12). Some priests prefer to take a good audio recording or book with them, as they go away to pray, perhaps in a religious or monastic institution. They might even have the opportunity to speak with one of the monks there. Others take advantage of the formation offered by the diocese or institutions in the Church designed to assist priests in their spiritual life through retreats and spiritual direction.

Some retreat masters will present certain themes like prayer, service, liturgy, and charity—while others give a more broad perspective of priesthood in the context of the Church and her message today. But whatever the format he chooses, the priest needs to make sure that the preacher will give ideas that are faithful to the Church's doctrines, and that present well the beauty and challenges of modern priesthood. The yearly retreat is also a perfect opportunity to make a general confession of sins and omissions over the previous year, to obtain more grace to go forward.

Let us conclude by going to Mary the Mother of Jesus, and Mother of all priests. It is true to say that we are her work and special responsibility. In union with her Son, she intercedes to God the Father for us always. She is aware of our temptations and failures, but she is also aware of the great mission that we are asked to carry out, as priests of her Son, and yes, as other Christs. When we say Mass, hear Confessions, and celebrate the other sacraments, she surely sees her Son working within us, which increases her love for us. Let us not neglect to ask Mary to help us each day in our work, and to sanctify that work for the glory of God and the good of souls.

SERVING THE FAITHFUL

"I have called you by your name; you are mine" (*Is* 43:1). This phrase summarizes not only the life of Isaiah, but that of all the prophets. They dedicated themselves to the people of Israel by preaching to them bravely, warning them of the punishment to come for their infidelity, all the while calling them back tenderly to God and His Covenant. And God gave them the specific grace to do all three things, along with pronouncing many prophecies about the Messiah and how He would be the definitive Savior of Israel.

As priests of the New Testament, our role is also to serve our people, and to keep them true to the Catholic Faith. As in the times of Isaiah and Jeremiah, we must remind them of the danger of idols—whether that be career, popularity, or materialism. At times the idols can be more subtle, such as self-absorption and indifference in the things of God .But as priests we must ask the Holy Spirit for the grace and inspiration to address these dangers, and move our people to love the one true God and his Son—not other gods.

We received this important mission on the day that we were ordained. On that marvelous day we received a specific ontological configuration with Jesus Christ, High Priest and Head of the Church. "Through consecration, the priest receives a spiritual power as a gift which is a participation in the authority with which Jesus Christ, through His Spirit, guides the Church" (*DLM*, n. 2). Our ordination therefore was not a mere ceremony, nor the chance for many people to be glad and to congratulate us after many years in the seminary. It was the central event in our life, when we received a specific character in our souls configuring us to Christ Himself. It is something ontological that distinguishes us from the common priesthood of the faithful. This permanent character truly constitutes us as other Christs, as we saw in the first section, with the three-fold mission of teaching, governing, and sanctifying His people through His name and His power—especially by preaching the Word and administering the sacraments.

Oh Lord, thank you for that day when I lay prostrate on the ground before your altar, when the Bishop laid hands upon my ahead and anointed my hands with the holy oil, when I received this greatest gift which I did not deserve, poor man that I am! Let me never forget that marvelous day, and give thanks to you always for it...Gratias tibi, Deus, gratias tibi! May I never forget who I am, the "new man" that I became that day.

At the very center of the priesthood will always be the celebration of Holy Mass. This sacrifice is not only the source and summit of the Church's life; it is also the source and summit of the priest's life. It gives him the direction and energy that he needs each day to bring the world to Christ, and Christ to the world. The doxology "Through Him, and with Him, and in Him" concludes all the Eucharistic Prayers of the Mass, followed by the great Amen. It really summarizes what each priest must be and do. Through Christ, with Christ, and in Christ he must sanctify his daily life and bring Christ's kingdom to the world, beginning with the hearts and souls of those near to him. Pope Benedict XVI, in his address to students at Cologne on World Youth Day in 2005, described what happens at Mass as a kind of powerful fission in the depths of reality, or an "explosion of good." He went on to state that we enter into the "dynamic of Christ's self-giving" at every Eucharist, which we can apply to ourselves particularly as priest celebrants. Just as terrorists and other evil-doers spread destruction through their explosions, those who participate in the Mass spread goodness with an entirely different kind of explosion: that of hope and grace into people's lives.

***

At the very center of our ministry then is the Holy Sacrifice, but there are other sacraments as well. The hearing of Confessions, or the ministry of Reconciliation, is one of the greatest services we can offer to others. *What a privilege, Lord, to be positioned between you and that penitent—man or woman—who sincerely wants to return to you with a good and contrite Confession! May I be a good listener above all, and encourage each one with what he or she needs to hear! May I also have the gentle fortitude of asking the right questions to help each person make a complete and integral confession, as much as he or she can do in their circumstances at the moment. As the* Catechism of the Catholic Church *states, in Confession I am Judge, Father, Physician, and Shepherd. May I inspire each one to trust completely in your most Sacred Heart, who are delighted with every penitent who returns to you.*

The ministry of the Confessional is the most important ministry of all, after the Holy Mass. To exercise the power of the keys and to apply God's mercy has repercussions far beyond a single Confession, which may take a few minutes only, or longer if needed. For every good Confession brings truth to a world that is erring, hope to a world that is often barren and desolate, grace to a world that is lost, love to a world that is running from Love. Confession is the sacrament of peace and joy when it is done well, both on the part of the penitent and the priest. For this reason we should generously make ourselves available to hear confessions, at an hour that is convenient and reasonable for the faithful…and as often as needed.

At times it may be good to pray about the *way* we hear Confessions, since it is easy to fall into a kind of routine mentality, or to become superficial about it. Are we really helping people to make integral confessions, that is, to confess any unconfessed grave sins in number and kind—as far as they are able to do so? Is our tone of voice and manner in the confessional charitable and helpful to people, or do we tend to be rude or accusatory, which will turn away people, instead of drawing them closer to Christ? At times we may have to ask discreet yet clear questions about certain moral issues, such as attendance at Mass, family obligations, and matters of chastity. Some people have the tendency to skim over serious sins, or confess them very vaguely. With the help of the Holy Spirit and the Curé of Ars, we can truly serve our people by helping them to make sincere and complete confessions, and also by giving them clear and encouraging advice. It may even be helpful to consult a classic manual or other worthwhile publication about the sacrament of Reconciliation, and how to administer it more effectively. Without violating the seal, we could also discuss things with an experienced and holy priest in order to learn more about how to deal with certain moral issues, to give better advice, and to increase our effectiveness as good confessors.

By increasing the number of people confessing their sins—young, old, and in the middle—the parish will be renewed, perhaps even revolutionized. That was the experience of Saint John Mary Vianney, and that is the experience of all good priests who truly love and practice faithfully the sacrament of Penance. "It is the priest who continues the work of redemption on earth," Saint John Mary affirms. "….What use would be a house filled with gold, were there no one to open its door? The priest holds the key to the treasures of heaven; it is he who opens the door…." (Translated from l'Abbe Bernard Nodet, *Le Curé d'Ars. Sa pensée—Son Coeur, 1966, pp.98-100*).

And of course, continuing in the message of the Year of the Priest, we particularly want to imitate the holy Curé and his sacrifice for souls in the Confessional, remembering his famous words: The priesthood is the love of the heart of Jesus (see *CCC*, n.1589).

***

That constant love and the work of glorifying God and serving others continues through all the other sacraments as well. Baptism forgives the guilt of original sin, brings a person into the Body of Christ, makes him a participant in the Divine Life of the Trinity, and creates an indelible character within the soul marking him or her as a child of God. When we stop to think of all this, one word comes to mind: Amazing! Let's pray that we will never get used to the mystery of it all, though we may have to do many baptisms in our life. Each is unique and irreplaceable, as well as an excellent opportunity for catechesis—for the parents, godparents, and all present. We can help them appreciate the greatness of Baptism and the Catholic Church, and instruct them to be especially faithful to that Church both as individuals and as spiritual guardians for the newly baptized child.

A large part of a priest's work is witnessing marriages and preparing couples for that great sacrament. Though we priests can be disappointed by the superficiality of many couples today, or even by more serious matters like co-habitation before Matrimony, we cannot give up our effort to instruct, correct, and encourage. A priest should be clear when he explains to them the purpose of Holy Matrimony— a life of mutual support and fidelity to one another, with openness to having and raising children. Though often married couples are involved in Pre-Cana programs, the priest can have a unique effect on the couple when he speaks to them about sacrifice and understanding for one another, the importance of prayer together, and the need to be open to children. They must know that any form of contraception is a grave sin against God's law for marriage, and against their own dignity as persons. He should do his best to make sure that the couple is in the state of grace when they receive Matrimony, since it is a sacrament of the living. And to some couples, who appear to be open to a more spiritual message, he could even speak of marriage as a path of holiness: that is, that each one, husband and wife, must help the other to get to heaven. This is the truest and most important goal of all Christian marriages, since the man and woman's relationship should be modeled on Christ's love for the Church, His bride (cf *Eph* 5). His homily at the wedding Mass or nuptial service can reiterate some of these important points, which would be good for all the attendees to hear even if they are not Catholic.

Likewise the anointing of the sick is a moment of grace, for not only the person in need but also the entire family and extended family. The moments surrounding death can lead to authentic conversions on the part of children or grandchildren who have been away from the Church for a long time. In caring for a sick or dying relative, their own hearts expand, and they wake up to the reality of human life and how quickly it passes. But above all, of course, the anointing of the sick brings grace and forgiveness to the ailing person, who is thus prepared for eternity. It is one of the most beautiful and consoling actions that a priest can do for others, and certainly one of the most satisfying of his works.

The *Directory* sums up the life and work of a priest in a very expressive way in n.14: "Called to an act of supernatural love, absolutely gratuitous, the priest should love the Church as Christ has loved her, consecrating to her all his energies and giving himself with pastoral charity in a continuous act of generosity." This love is expressed not only in giving the sacraments, as seen above, but in many other little ways. It is expressed in our tone of voice, which should be positive and encouraging with people, and in our availability to help them even if we ourselves are inconvenienced. Like good professionals, we should be on time for things. It is a lack of charity and even of competence to keep people waiting. Therefore we should be punctual in fulfilling our commitments: the celebration of Mass, the hearing of Confessions, counseling sessions, committee meetings, etc. In all these matters we are living courtesy and charity to those who are waiting for us.

***

A dedicated priest will also prepare his talks and homilies well. They should not only be true to the Church's authentic Magisterium but also should move and inspire the faithful. "Dynamic fidelity" is the expression that Pope John Paul II once used in speaking with American priests about preaching; the homilist's words must be faithful to what Christ taught and what the Church has always taught—yet have a dynamism and appeal that will move people to be better and do better. He should not avoid the harder issues in his homilies, such as the wrongness of contraception and sterilization, the obligation to go to Mass on Sundays, the existence of mortal sin, the importance of sacramental confession, and the reality of the afterlife—death, judgment, heaven, and hell. In preaching about these things he is being faithful both to the Gospel and the perennial teachings of the Church, which have been guided by the Holy Spirit over the centuries. He is also being fair to his people; they have a right to hear the whole truth of Revelation, which comes from God's love for us. It would be wrong for us to preach only of God's Mercy and never of His Justice. We may reasonably affirm that many people over the centuries have been saved because they heard clearly from their priest what was a grave sin and what was hell—and they knew how to avoid both. It takes effort to find the appropriate phrases and approaches for these topics, but it will be a great support to the faithful, who must live in a materialistic and relativist environment that is often opposed to moral ideals and objective truths.

Oh Lord, help me to find good sources for my homily—either from books, or online ideas, or simply good stories from my brother priests. And when I go to the pulpit, may I speak about you—your life and the teachings of your Church—not my own private experiences or theories about things. I'm not there to communicate dissent from your Church, but love and unity with her.

Part of a priest's work is administrative, often more than he wishes. He will have meetings to attend, such as with the parish council and other groups; he will have paperwork to forward to the diocesan offices; he will have other forms to fill out concerning marriages, baptisms, possible annulment proceedings. If he is pastor, he will have many checks to sign and be responsible for coordinating parish spending. There will also be fundraising and certain kinds of administration for which he has not been trained in the seminary. All of these things can be quite frustrating at times for some priests, especially those who do not have an organizational mentality. But since it is part of his work, this too can be made holy if done with the right intention. "Seeing God and souls in papers" is an old saying that has a lot of value in these cases. The Lord in the Gospel teaches: "If any man would come after Me, let him deny himself and take up his cross and follow Me" (*Mt* 16:24). Often that cross will be a big folder of papers on our desk, a stack of phone messages, a computer system that has broken down, or an emergency meeting for which we are unprepared. *Oh Lord help me to remember that in all of these things I must take up my cross, without complaining. Though I receive neither good feelings nor sense of reward by doing them, I know that I am serving you in this way. I offer up my extra work and the trials of the day for vocations to the priesthood, and for the souls in Purgatory."*

***

So much of a priest's work, including administration and paperwork, can be summarized in one word: LOVE The *Directory* has a rather lengthy but very deep description of this principle of love in all the works of the priest: "Pastoral charity constitutes the internal and dynamic principle capable of uniting the multiple and diverse pastoral activities of the priest and, given the socio-cultural and religious context in which he lives, is an indispensable instrument for drawing men to a life in Grace" (*DLM*, n.43) .To put the whole thing very simply, priesthood is the love of the heart of Jesus, as we saw above from the Cure of Ars.

Our work therefore can never be that of a mere functionary. If we don't have a strong life of prayer, if we don't rectify our intention frequently, we can easily see our job as mainly bureaucratic, as filling a kind of job description in the diocese, not as a priest of Jesus Christ ordained to save souls. We said above that activism is a big danger for all of us, including lay people. We can become very busy about parish or diocesan activities, but lose our spirit of prayer and reflection. Our work would become sterile then, like the barren fig tree in the Gospel. *Oh Lord, help me to see my work always as a way to love you and give glory to you, and as a way to serve your people! Help me to dedicate time to prayer each day, and to say frequent aspirations to you, so that I don't see my work as mere busyness, and forget its true purpose.*

What the Church needs most today—now more than ever, after the scandals involving priests and bishops that have racked her over the last decade—are faithful and holy priests who work hard. Hopefully they will not look at themselves in their priesthood as "climbers," that is, as those who calculate everything they say or do in order to please certain people, or get attention so that they can ascend the ecclesiastical ladder. They should not be career priests but Christ's priests. They should not be whiners or complainers who see only problems or obstacles; blaming others for the state of the Church and society is a very sterile and useless frame of mind. With humility, we must simply get to work and be the best priests of Jesus Christ that that we can be. "The son of man came not to be served, but to serve" (*Mt* 20:28), said Christ the High Priest and model for all of us. Or, to use the words of John the Baptist referring to the Messiah, "He must increase, but I must decrease" (*Jn* 3:30).

In short, holy, hard-working priests will be an indispensable part of the leaven that renews the Church from within, and ultimately changes society. As we try to serve the Church and sanctify our work, a marvelous patron for all priests is that hard-working humble man named Saint Joseph. He is truly the head of the household, who protects and leads Mother and Child. He fulfills his vocation in a personal and responsible way. Besides being a model for all fathers of families, he is a model for all of us priests who are also fathers. We too must lead others to God; we too must be men of prayer and purity, who know how to offer our work to God each day in union with Christ. Saint Joseph can teach us, in his silent unassuming way, how to be true to our vocation and to serve the Church. As Patron of the Universal Church, he can win us the grace to love the sacraments more, especially as we serve our people the Bread of Life. "Father, with unselfish love St. Joseph cared for your Son, born of the Virgin Mary. May we also serve at your altar with pure hearts. We ask this in the name of Jesus the Lord" (Prayer over the Gifts, *Mass for the Solemnity of Saint Joseph*, March 19th).

***

Saint Josemaria Escrivá, whose life and work have helped millions of Catholics, both priests and lay faithful, to find God in their daily work once wrote that "man's great privilege is to be able to love and to transcend what is fleeting and ephemeral. He can love other creatures, pronounce an "I" and "you" which are full of meaning….This is why man ought not to limit himself to material production. Work is born of love; it is a manifestation of love and is directed toward love. We see the hand of God, not only in the wonders of nature, but also in our experience of work and effort" (*Christ is Passing By,* n.48 , Scepter Publishers, New York). Priests and lay faithful are therefore called to give God glory in their daily work, and indeed to be co-redeemers with Christ himself. As priests our pastoral work is particularly united to Jesus' own action in souls, as we administer the sacraments, preach, and give spiritual direction to others.

In all of these things let's avoid the temptation of the "spectacular." This was the content of two of the devil's propositions to Christ during his forty day fast…that is, to turn the stones into bread for His own benefit, and to cast Himself from the top of the Temple. He can similarly undermine our dedication as priests—tempting us to view priesthood as a way of personal satisfaction, or as a way of being praised and highly regarded by our contemporaries. He can also insinuate that we would be much happier doing something else, in a different diocese, in a different parish, thereby leaving us unhappy in our present condition. To counteract these temptations, we will need to have more faith and trust in God's providence: God wants me right now in *this* assignment, in *this* Church or parish, with *these* people, and therefore I will serve them as best as I can. I will look at my work each day and try to sanctify it by completing it conscientiously, in the big things and little things, with a spirit of service and love. *Lord, give me this operative faith, by which I believe in your will for me in this work that I am doing, here and now. Help me to avoid wishful thinking or escapisms that put me in dream worlds: wait until I get that parish, wait until I'm a Monsignor, wait until my vacation to Florida, wait until there's a new bishop. It's all wishful and wasteful thinking that takes me from my real work of each day. Lord, give me more faith in the help of your grace in my daily life.*

We also need to exercise <u>hope</u> in our ministry. Christ does work through me as a priest, despite my sinfulness and miseries. No grace is ever lost, no work is ever useless if it is done for the love of God and of others. *Even if I have spent a long time trying to convert others to the Faith, or to bring back wavering or distant Catholics, without apparent success, I must have supernatural hope in God's grace. I must always remember St. Paul's timeless insight: "We know that in everything God works for good with those who love Him…" (Rom 8:28).*

The kingdom of God is indeed like a small lump of leaven; it works silently and mysteriously, but in the end it ferments the whole mass of dough and lifts up the bread, making it substantial and nutritious. Isn't the quiet persevering work of a good priest like that?

Our Lady's silent prayer and work helped to redeem the world, in union with Saint Joseph and her Son. How often she would be praying for his disciples, and for all the men and women who were coming closer to Him, listening to His words and being healed by Him. Let's entrust our flock very much to her care. She is the mother of the Church, and can intercede in a most personal and powerful way for those in need. *Remember O Most Gracious Virgin Mary…*

HUMILITY

"And to keep me from being too elated by the abundance of revelations, a thorn was given me in the flesh, a messenger of Satan, to harass me, to keep me from being too elated" (*II Cor* 12:7). The apostle had just written of certain special favors that God had given him, including great success in the apostolate, and yet now he reveals that he has to suffer a certain humiliation. Some scholars think that it could have been a sickness, maybe malaria picked up in the swamps of Pamphilia; others think that it could have been the constant opposition that he had to endure from those of his own flesh, the Jews; and still others think it could have been a strong temptation or obsessive desire against chastity. But the main point of the text is Paul's response to his situation. He prays to the Lord three times to remove the thorn, but He does not take it away. So St.Paul ends up by embracing it, and even giving God praise for it: "I will all the more gladly boast of my weaknesses, that the power of Christ may rest upon me....for when I am weak, then I am strong" (*II Cor* 12: 9.10).

What a magnificent spirit, Lord, does the Apostle have! May I have the same reaction when I see my obvious weaknesses and failings; rather than despair about them, will trust you all the more. You can turn my wretchedness into the victory, and that of others as well.

Humility is an essential virtue for becoming a saint. It is the ultimate realism that makes us see how little we are, and how great God is. The humble person is a man of truth; he does not exaggerate either his virtues or his defects, and he recognizes that all he has is really a gift. As Father Canals states in his charming little book, *Jesus as Friend* (Four Courts Press, Dublin, 1986, p.35): "True humility begins at the bright point where the mind discovers and admits, sufficiently clearly for the heart to be able to love it, the simple, deep, basic truth that 'without me you can do nothing'" (cf *Jn* 15:5).

Humility therefore is a virtue of both mind and will. Our mind recognizes the truth of our littleness and dependence, and our will accepts this, and even loves it. With this attitude the Holy Spirit can truly build upon our priesthood. We will appreciate the need to pray continually, not trusting in our own strength or personality; we will be prompt to obey the will of our superiors, without emphasizing our own preferences; we will be able to see the needs of others, because we are not submerged in our own needs or problems.

***

It is clearly pride, or ego, that ruins everything. As one Catholic psychologist put it, ego means Edging God Out. Pride or self-absorption puts us in a world of personal concerns or resentments where no one can enter—like a man enclosing himself in a dark dingy room and refusing to open the window for the sun or fresh air. It leads us to oversensitivity where we are constantly judging or condemning others, whether they be our parishioners, fellow priests, or the bishop. The prideful man refuses to be corrected and wants always to be the center of attention; as a result he ends up disliked and miserable. "Be sure, my friend," says Father Canals, "that almost always the cause of our ups and downs and of our restlessness lies in excessive concern over our self-esteem or a desire to be highly regarded by others. The humble soul puts self-esteem and others' regard into God's hands" (*Jesus as Friend*, p.37).

Real humility will therefore lead a priest to find a good spiritual guide for his soul. He recognizes his own weakness and blindness, and the need to have a friend and a brother who knows him well and can truly help him to become a holy priest. Our spiritual director should be a person of sound Catholic doctrine, holiness of life, experience in directing souls, and someone capable of demanding things of us. Let's not worry that somehow we will lose our freedom in opening up to another, or lose our personality. With consistent and effective direction, our personality will become enriched in Christ, and we will obtain freedom from egotism, laziness, and self-deception. It helps if we have personal rapport or "good chemistry" in speaking with our spiritual director, but it's not necessary. The most important thing is that he understands us and pray for us; this is the man who will truly help us to become saints.

One of the best ways to grow in humility is to make a good examination of conscience every day. With the help of the Holy Spirit and our guardian angel, we need to look at our day objectively—giving thanks for God's blessings and the good actions we have done, and making an act of contrition for our sins and faults. By making a daily examination of conscience—perhaps at Compline or Night Prayer—we can refer our entire life to God: we recognize that all the good things in our day are really His gifts, but that the sins of our day come from our own weakness and lack of love for Him.

Part of humility in any man is to recognize what we can call our predominant fault. Our predominant fault is the result of Original Sin that each of us has inherited, and it usually has different manifestations in our life. For some of us it may be pridefulness, mentioned above, which makes us overly sensitive and self-absorbed, and which can lead to stubbornness and vanity. It leads us to compare ourselves to other priests, and to be overly concerned with our image or reputation in others' eyes. For some others it may be anger or impatience, that is, wanting instant results from persons and things around us, and not knowing how to wait. Related to anger is sarcasm, giving into bad moods and uncharitable speech. For still others of us our predominant fault may be laziness, which is the tendency to do the minimum in our duties and put off things. Because of this fault we don't pray as we should, we skip parts of the Breviary or excuse ourselves too easily from it, we don't prepare talks and homilies well, we don't care for our people as we should. We can even excuse ourselves from our duties by saying that we are very busy—committee meetings, travel, diocesan programs, etc—but we have really fallen into a kind of *acedia*, which is a slothfulness or sadness in performing the things of the spirit.

With humility we can also recognize in ourselves a certain attachment to material things. Though we are priests and are supposed to be leading simple humble lives, we live in a materialistic world where there is great emphasis on the car we drive, where we go on vacation, how many electronic gadgets we have. It's easy for us to become attached to these things and even to consider our worth by how many things we have compared to others. This sort of attitude can only have a negative effect on our prayer life and can often be a cause of scandal to the faithful or to our brother priests. Finally there is sensuality, or excessive attachment to the pleasures of the flesh. This includes overeating, comfort seeking, and the abuse of alcohol. It also includes of course sins against chastity, whether with ourselves or with another. In our modern age the internet is a big source of temptation and sin against the Sixth Commandment, and can lead to real addictions that can enslave the soul and deeply hurt our priesthood, even our manhood.

In all these areas we need to be honest with ourselves, which is part of humility. Let's not forget the famous words of Pope Pius XII after World War II: "The greatest sin of the 20th century has been the loss of the sense of sin." With much of modern psychology justifying sin and abnormal behaviors, it is easy for us to explain away or excuse ourselves and others from a brave and honest examination of our lives. Or, as said above, we can invent many reasons to avoid praying and reflecting on the real truth, or non-truth, of our lives. For all of these motives we need to make frequent acts of contrition. There is no need to wait for the day of our Confession to make an act of contrition and atonement. When we recognize our sinfulness, let's say right away: "Lord, have mercy on me, a sinner"; or "Father, forgive me"; or "My God, I am heartily sorry for having offended you"; or, in the words of the repentant Peter, "Lord, you know all things; you know that I love you" (Jn 21:17). In this way we will not become depressed at our falls, or carry behind us a trail of miseries all day long. Like the prodigal son, we will cast ourselves into the merciful arms of God the Father and begin again as often as we need to. The best motive of our contrition is of course the love of God, who is all good, and who has given us our life, the Catholic Faith, and our priesthood. Certainly we fear the punishment of Purgatory and Hell, but above all we are sorry for having offended such a good God by our pridefulness, anger, laziness, or comfort seeking. We should make many acts of contrition each day for this motive, and encourage our people to do the same.

If we are humble, and examine our conscience regularly, we will feel the need for frequent Confession also. "Like any good faithful, the priest also needs to confess his own sins and weaknesses. He is the first to realize that the practice of this sacrament reinforces his faith and charity toward God and his brothers" (*DLM*, n.53). Pope John Paul II put it even more dramatically: "….the entire priestly existence falls into decay if there is lacking, through neglect or for any other motive, the periodic recourse, inspired by true faith and devotion, to the Sacrament of Penance" (Post-Synodal Apostolic Exhortation *Reconciliatio et Paenitentia* (December 1984), n.31). Of course, if we have been unfortunate enough to commit a grave sin, we should go to Confession as soon as possible, for the good of our own souls, and to be able to celebrate the sacraments worthily. But even in the case of venial sins or imperfections, let's take frequent advantage of the sacrament of forgiveness and grace. Humility and love for God grows with every sincere sacramental Confession we make. In this way we can identify much more with the penitents who come to us, since we know that we are poor sinners also. We can also obtain a specific sacramental grace to improve our lives, and draw closer to the Good Shepherd Himself. "For I came not to call the righteous, but sinners" (*Mt* 9:13).

With humble self-knowledge we also recognize the need for a continuing formation to be good priests. It would be a lack of humility for us to think that we've received sufficient formation already in the seminary, and that after ordination or after our first appointment as Pastor we do not need growth in faith, prayer life, or virtue. Or we could think that we only need training in administration or fund-raising, but not in spiritual matters. The truth is that we can always improve in our spiritual life. For this reason we should avail ourselves of seminars on Church teachings and current moral issues, conferences on preaching styles, reflections on priesthood, and certainly recollections or retreats that will challenge us to a deeper life of prayer and virtue. Saint Bernard of Clairvaux once told his brother religious: "The man who stops wanting to become better ceases to be good." These are words that apply to men of all centuries, both ordained and the lay faithful.

Let's be eager for improvement and correction always. We can all fail in big or little areas in the way we say Mass, in the way we preach, in the way we deal with others. If we receive a correction from a brother priest, a superior, or a member of the lay faithful—let's be grateful to those people and humbly take their correction or observation to our prayer. If we recognize that we are ignorant about some point of liturgy or theology, we can consult a sound book or seek appropriate advice.

We should also ask ourselves frequently if we are completely sincere with our spiritual director or confessor. Pridefulness likes to hide things, and to make us appear better than we really are. In our sessions with our spiritual director, we need to be open about our faults, and even say the *hardest thing first*. Msgr. Escrivá used to advise people to "get rid of the big stones first" in spiritual direction, that is, to speak of those issues that weigh on us more heavily or that are harder to talk about. With sincerity we can get to the roots of our faults. For instance, it would be a waste of time for a priest to speak about his intellectual endeavors or readings with his spiritual director while never mentioning his falls in chastity. Similarly, it would be foolish for a priest to speak a long time about liturgical issues but never reveal his deep anger or frustration with a fellow priest or parishioner. With true humility, therefore, we learn to be sincere; that is, according to the Latin etymology of that word, we have "no wax" (*sine cera*) or cover-up in our conversations. In this way we can really be helped in Confession and spiritual direction; God's grace can penetrate our souls, and we will feel much happier and liberated in the end.

***

We priests are here to serve, following Christ's own self-description: He came not to be served, but to serve (cf *Mt* 20:28). We were ordained as God's ministers to praise and give glory to Him, to serve His Church, to care for His flock, and, if necessary, to give our lives for them. We did not become priests for people to notice us or praise us, to call us teacher or "father," or to be esteemed by society. If we do receive promotions in the Church, such as to be named Monsignor or receive a higher office, we look at them only as opportunities to serve the Church more, with an added responsibility. And we pray for the grace to continue serving, without vanity or pridefulness, in that new position. "O Jesus, may I be the last in everything, and the first in Love" (Saint Josemaria, *The Way*, n.430).

Obedience is closely connected with humility. The humble priest actually desires to obey, not only because of his vow to the Ordinary but also because he distrusts himself and sincerely wants to be guided. He listens carefully to the indications of his bishop or superior, even if he must go against the grain sometimes and change his plans. In preaching to his people, he follows the authentic teachings of the Catholic Church and does not change them or invent his own ideas in order to receive more notoriety or attention. He follows the promptings of the Holy Spirit in his life of prayer and sacrifice. And if he has a doubt on any of his ideas or plans, he checks them promptly with his spiritual director, to whom he has entrusted the command of his spiritual ship. As mentioned before, he is open to correction, either from his fellow priests or lay persons, realizing that he has many faults, including those that he cannot see. Consequently, the humble priest is easy to approach and to talk to; people do not have to be on guard with him, because they know that he is open and understanding.

One of the dangers of ministry is the sin of vanity, which is certainly related to pridefulness: "Pride really is nothing other than a disordered evaluation of one's qualities and talents. It is nothing but the blown-up and disordered idea that we have formed of ourselves" (*Jesus as Friend*, p.46). We can be tempted to become vain if people compliment us, as they often will do with very good intentions, in order to encourage us in our vocation. "O Father, what a beautiful liturgy! O Father, what a moving homily! O Father, how well you handled that family in their grief!" In those moments and others, when vanity leads us to congratulate ourselves, we need to say "*Deo omnis Gloria!*" To God all the glory! If we have done well, it is because of His grace and the Holy Spirit working within us.

We said before that etymologies can help us to understand the meaning of key virtues in our lives. The word humility actually comes from the Latin word *humus*, meaning "mound of earth." We as priests speak of Heaven, but we must have our feet firmly planted on the ground. We cannot separate ourselves from the daily cares and chores of this life, or the daily cares and chores of our people, even if we have a high position in a parish or the diocese. For this reason it is good for us to do simple humble things each day for others. Christ's washing the feet of His disciples was not only for dramatic effect. It did indeed have dramatic effect—they never forgot it—but the message was greater than the drama. It showed the profound truth of humility and real service which the apostles must have for one another, and which *we* must have for one another.

Life is made up of simple, humble things. This of course was one of the great insights of Saint Therese of Lisieux and her *Little Way*, which has inspired millions of souls for over a hundred years. She had great ambitions to serve God and the Church as a missionary, as a teacher, a doctor, a martyr; but she learned that the offering of little things each day for the sake of love can also be heroic. "I realized that love sets off the bounds of all vocations, that love is everything, that this same love embraces every time and every place" (from her autobiography, Lisieux 1957, 227-229). In another passage she compares herself to a little rubber ball that Jesus could throw around and step on, but that she would not complain, as long as she was pleasing Him. *O Lord, at times as a priest I feel like a rubber ball, with so many things to do, and people to serve, and diocesan matters to attend to…I never get a rest! But let me see the value of the little things of each day, which are for your glory, and I will not lose my peace.* With humility, we learn to be constant in our duties, to say our Breviary well, to be punctual to our appointments, to get up on time, to keep smiling even to people who annoy us. This is the way to true humility and true happiness, both at the beginning and end of our journey.

The greatest woman, the greatest human person who ever lived, once described herself as a handmaid—the handmaid of the Lord. She saw her whole life in terms of service, so that He who was mighty could do great things in her (cf. *Lk* 1:49). She had no pretensions; she put no obstacles to the grace of the Holy Spirit coming into her. Such was the way that Mary of Nazareth literally brought God to the world, with a hope that will never fade for all of us human beings. As priests let's humbly ask our Mother to obtain the grace of humility for us, so indispensable for our lives and ministry.

SUPERNATURAL HOPE AND OPTIMISM

"What shall we say to this? If God is for us, who is against us? He who did not spare his own Son but gave Him up for us all, will He not also give us all things with Him?" (*Rom* 8:31-32). Saint Paul's magnificent words resound throughout the centuries, especially in our hearts as priests. The great virtue of hope is a result of God's infinite love for us; it gives us the ability to trust in His promise to us and to keep us advancing on the path to holiness. It is very much connected with the awareness of our divine filiation, namely, that we are sons of God and part of His Divine Family. We are also His priests, and therefore inserted into the power of Christ the High Priest.

It's easy to fall into a rather lukewarm and comfortable view of priesthood, which could take many forms: "Do the minimum possible," "Don't make waves," "Just wait for the next vacation time." Such views, even if they exist only in our subconscious thoughts, can undermine our dedication and, ultimately, our hope in God's grace. For if there is no struggle to be better, what is there to hope for in the end? Our life could easily fall into mediocrity and even despair. Michelangelo, great Renaissance sculptor and painter of the Sistine Chapel in the Vatican, once wrote: "The problem with most people is not that they aim too high, and fail; the problem is that they aim too low, and succeed."

Let's aim high, at least as high as many lay people who want to become millionaires, or leaders in society. Our goal is to reach eternal life and to enjoy God's company forever, and as far as we can, to bring thousands of people with us. That includes people such as our relatives, our fellow priests, our parishioners, our friends. These are the goals of a true man of God, who makes prayer, charity, and the sacraments the very center of his life. All the great saints had a source of hope and joy within them that the world could not give. For this reason they were able to persevere, and even smile, in the face of countless adversities. When he was told by his bishop about the sorry spiritual state of Ars before he went there, Saint John Mary immediately prayed: "Lord, grant me the conversion of my parish; I am willing to suffer whatever you wish, for my entire life" (Nodet, p.183).

Each of us received the supernatural virtue of hope, along with faith and charity, at our Baptism. We also received—both priests and laymen—the capacity to trust in God's promises despite the disappointments and trials of our life on earth. Since it comes from God, hope endures and will ultimately lead us to victory. It is something that we say at every Mass in the Preface: Sursum Corda! Lift up your hearts! This brief encouraging aspiration not only prepares us and the faithful for the miracle of the Consecration, but also for the various events the day will bring. Since we are God's people, his sons and daughters, we have a basically positive and optimistic view of people and events—but without being naïve.

Jesus told His apostles that He was going to prepare a place for them in His Father's house (cf *Jn* 14:2). Our real goal, the purpose of our lives, is to reach eternal life, to enjoy God and His Love forever. To this end we sincerely try to become saints on this earth and to spread God's Kingdom on earth as much as possible. This is the task that we priests and the lay faithful share, each in our own way.

***

To have hope, I repeat, means to aim high. "For where your treasure is, there will your heart be also" (*Mt* 6:21). Our treasure as priests should be in administering the sacraments, in preaching the Word of God convincingly, in assisting our brothers and sisters in the Church to find eternal life. In many ways our treasure must also be in the cross of Christ, where we can unite our sacrifice with His, and thus bring His saving grace to the world. One of our most important missions is to give people hope, even though society and other people, including family members, at times will give them very little of it. Pope John Paul II in his apostolic letter on the New Millenium proposed this Gospel message as the direction of the Church for the years ahead: *Duc in altum*, put out into the deep (cf *Lk* 5:4). Then he stated that the pursuit of holiness must be the first pastoral goal of the Church. We priests must animate and encourage the faithful, including at times our brother priests who might be saddened or burdened by the cares of life; we must urge them to look with hope at God's providence and to continue forward. Pope Benedict XVI said something very similar to the youth of Australia in 2008: "Through the Spirit's action may the young people gathered here have the courage to become saints! This is what the world needs more than anything else" (Government House Ceremony, July 16, 2008).

Christian hope is not something sugary or the foolish idea that things will take care of themselves and turn out fine. We are very much aware of sin in our lives, and in others, with the sad consequence that things can often go from bad to worse—in families, in countries, in personal relationships. Such things increase our realism but should not dampen our supernatural hope. If Christ the man and His apostles failed to hope, there would be no Church in the first place, and the world would have fallen more and more into paganism and, ultimately, into the hands of Satan. No, the spirit of a Christian is to face problems and to keep struggling, valiantly, until the end. He does not run away or give up trying to be good—though he receives little recognition or reward for it.

I recall in this respect a story from the life of Saint Josemaría Escrivá, the founder of Opus Dei. At the beginning of the Spanish Civil Way, in 1936, he and the first members of the Work had to keep in hiding, to avoid being killed by anti-Catholic anarchists and communists who had seized control of the city. At last they were able to find refuge, with many others, in the Legation of Honduras since it offered international immunity. Although their quarters were extremely cramped, as was their food supply, St. Josemaria inspired those first members to have hope, and to dream of the expansion of Opus Dei after the war was over. He even got them to study languages of different countries, where Opus Dei would begin centers some day. He obviously had a supernatural hope that he was able to communicate to those few young fellows, who wanted to give themselves completely to God. And so they studied German, Japanese, and Russian, though they couldn't even go out to the streets!

***

We were made for eternal life. We are destined to rule the universe with the angels and saints under the headship of Christ the King. In the words of Pope Benedict to young people, which we quoted in the first section: "Life is not governed by chance; it is not random. Your very existence has been willed by God, blessed and given a purpose! Life is not just a succession of events or experiences. It is a search for the true, the good, and the beautiful."

One of our central obligations as priests, therefore, is to give people hope. In a materialistic world, it is very easy for them to be caught up by material things, or a life of pleasure. There are many means of gratification in our society, and many of them simply enslave people… such as excessive drinking, greed, or illicit sexual experience. But the worst consequence of materialism is that people have little knowledge of what really matters in life. Since their view is glued to the ground, they cannot see the stars. As a result they really have little to live for, or to die for. Without the knowledge of truth, their lives can become empty and without meaning. For this reason, there are many who are depressed in life, and seem to be paralyzed. To all these people we have to say with Saint Paul: "You did not receive the spirit of slavery to fall back into fear, but you have received the spirit of sonship. When we cry, 'Abba! Father!' it is the Spirit Himself bearing witness with our spirit that we are children of God…" (*Rom* 8:15-16).

Hope, as we see, is very much connected with trust. The more we trust, and really believe, that a good and merciful God is in control of our lives, and of the world, the more hopeful we shall be. But if we give in to pessimism, which always sees the worst side of people or events, we cannot see grace working in the world—like a man in a dark room who refuses to open the curtains. In some ways it is easy to be negative or pessimistic, because we can convince ourselves that it is not worth trying anymore. But if we consider often and live the great fact of our divine sonship, we will live with abandonment and trust in God who is a loving father, even when things do not go our way, and there is suffering, and even tragedy. "I can do all things in Him who strengthens me...for when I am weak, then I am strong" (*Phil* 4:13; II Cor 12:10).

The Holy Spirit has a lot to do with hope and its brother, courage. We recall how the apostles awaited anxiously for the coming of the third Person in the upper room in Jerusalem. Perhaps many of them felt fearful and paralyzed at the great mission that Jesus had given them before His Ascension: "Go therefore and make disciples of all nations" (*Mt* 28:19). Most of them were fishermen who had not traveled beyond the borders of Israel. They did not have the culture of the Greeks, or the power of the Romans. What's more, their Master the Messiah had just been crucified, and as His disciples they felt they were marked men. They could easily be arrested at any time for having been His collaborators. Many of Christ's sayings they did not understand, and some may still have entertained doubts about the Resurrection itself (cf *Mt* 28:17). But then the great moment happened. The Holy Spirit came upon them, in the form of wind and tongues of fire, while they were at prayer. They received what we can only call supernatural hope and optimism to the highest degree.

Rather than being afraid to show themselves, now they went out to the streets proclaiming that Christ is truly God and the Messiah. Nothing had really changed in the world before the coming of the Holy Spirit. What had changed were the hearts of the apostles. They had received the gift of fortitude and courage: no matter what the obstacles, they knew that they would win in the battle for souls. They had received an answer to their doubts, and understood many more things about Christ and His Church. And it was that hope that was passed on to the early Christians and to all of us, throughout the centuries: "It is not the elemental spirits of the universe, the laws of matter, which ultimately govern the world and mankind, but a personal God governs the stars, that is the universe" (*Spe Salvi*, n.5).

***

We too have been given the Holy Spirit, not only in Baptism and Confirmation but also at our priestly ordination. The Holy Spirit filled us with his gifts of understanding, counsel, piety and fortitude to help us give glory to God and to minister to our people. Despite the obstacles in ourselves and others, we must not be afraid, and like the apostles, we will proclaim the truth and love of Jesus Christ bravely. Yes, with the help of the Paraclete we priests are called to give people hope, just as Christ did when he said that they were the light of the world, and that they should be holy, as their heavenly Father is holy (cf *Mt* 5:14.48). He didn't let them fall into mediocre or pessimistic thinking. In our relationships with people, of all backgrounds and situations, let's learn how to motivate them and give them encouragement. Even if we must speak of sin, we can always finish by speaking of the great sacrament of Confession, which is also the sacrament of grace and hope. God will always give us another chance if we are truly sorry for our sins.

But a world without God, without sin and forgiveness, without ideals and the need to sacrifice for those ideals—is a very sad and ultimately *boring* world. All of us priests must have an enduring supernatural trust in the Church. Despite our own sins and those of others, Christ's marvelous promise remains: "Lo, I am with you always, to the close of the age" (*Mt* 28:20). The Church cannot fail since she is the Bride of Christ; and we priests will not fail if we serve this Bride loyally. The sacraments continue to give grace and hope to the world throughout the centuries, and we priests are the ministers of those sacraments. We are men of hope when we say "I baptize you," "I absolve you," and all the other formulas of the sacraments. We are men of hope in the most excellent way when we say the words of consecration: This is my Body. This is my Blood.

Good preaching also gives positive motivation. If we are true to the meaning of Scripture, as given life and power by the Holy Spirit in the Church, we can do great good for people. We can make the Scriptures come alive, and give individuals the encouragement and motivation that they need for their families, friends, and work. Even if we are blind, we can ask Christ to let us see (cf *Lk* 18:41). If we are lepers, He can make us clean with one word (cf *Mt* 8:2). If we believe in Christ, we can do great things for our friends (cf *Mk* 2:5). We need to be deeply convinced that we are called, each one of us, to become a saint and be an apostle of hope to those around us. Let's pray and prepare our talks and homilies well, so that the Holy Spirit can use us as instruments to spread His daring joyfulness to our people.

***

Many times we ourselves must beg for the virtue of hope. Financial problems, difficulties in the parish, our own faults and weaknesses, lack of people's appreciation for us (or so we think) can get us down—along perhaps with the basic sameness of our lives day after day. Such are the moments to beg the Holy Spirit to increase our hope. As we saw before, it was the Holy Spirit who moved and stirred the apostles in the upper room on the feast of Pentecost. Yes, now they could overcome all obstacles and preach the truth which Christ had commissioned them to do. They experienced the real power and magnetism of the Gospel. In the insightful words of Pope Benedict, "the Gospel is not merely a communication of things that can be known—it is one that makes things happen and is life-changing. The dark door of time, of the future, has been thrown open. The one who has hope lives differently; the one who hopes has been granted the gift of a new life" (*Spe Salvi*, n.2).

So much of our hope comes from God's Truth. What most discourages people of our times is to live without seeing a purpose to their life. They can get along for a while, but eventually everyone must ask himself or herself: what is the meaning of it all? What is human nature, what is man, and who am I? Why is there suffering and evil in the world? With the help of God's wisdom and the Church's teachings, we can give them the answers to those questions. The deepest truth about ourselves and the meaning of human existence is that we are made in God's image and likeness, and that through grace we are called to be part of His Divine Family. For God so loved the world that He gave His only Son, that whoever believes in Him should not perish but have eternal life (*Jn* 3:16). Both truth and love combine to give us hope. But without experiencing that truth and love, we can easily pass through life in a depressed or semi-depressed condition, not really knowing where we are going or why. We may work hard, we may be very active, we may even do many good works for our fellow human beings as a humanitarian, but if we see no supernatural purpose to life, if we experience no love beyond human love—we are in darkness still.

The story of the Gospel is the story of people who felt themselves to be loved by Christ, and as result of that love, they received a purpose once again to their life. They received hope. A good part of hope is to begin again, as any baseball player will tell you who once again steps up to bat, in order to get a hit and possibly a home run. The Gospel is filled with people who received hope and began their lives again: Zachaeus the publican of Jericho, Mary Magdalene, from whom seven devils were expelled, poor Peter, who out of weakness had denied Christ several times. In some way these persons are like each one of us. Though we fall many times, though we have committed embarrassing, even heinous sins, we must sincerely repent and go back confidently to God and His Son. And we know that we are loved and given strength, always.

Let's foster a great devotion to Mary, our Hope. She is the one who brought Hope Himself to the world, and she never ceased trusting in His plan for her and the whole human race, despite the complete despair and desolation of the cross. If at times we feel very small and helpless, and even begin to feel the cold breath of sadness or cynicism rise within our souls, let's once again become small boys holding our mother's hand. "Before, by yourself, you couldn't," says Saint Josemaria. "Now you've turned to Our Lady, and with her, how easy" (Saint Josemaria Escrivá, *The Way*, n.513).

FIDELITY TO THE CHURCH

Who then is the faithful and wise servant, whom his master has set over his household, to give them their food at the proper time (*Mt* 24:45)? How greatly our Savior admired the virtue of fidelity. So many of His teachings and parables have to do with individuals who have made a commitment and are true to it—like the servants with the talents, the good shepherd, and the man who buys the field for the pearl of great price.

We as priests have also made a great commitment—to serve the Bride of Christ faithfully and to be true to the grace of our ordination. We are literally ordered to the Church, which includes her teachings, her sacraments, and the faithful who belong to her. Let's never shirk our duties, nor out of cowardice surrender to worldly views, giving the Church and her people less than they deserve. As priests we are part of the covenant between God and His people, which began in the various covenants of the Old Testament and culminated in Christ's Covenant of love on Calvary. During all those years God was true to His word, and we as his priests must be true to ours. Our Lord promised His Church that He would never abandon her, as the good spouse never abandons his beloved (cf *Mt* 28:20).

We are called to give ourselves completely to the Holy Catholic Church, despite the weakness and sinfulness of her members—our own included. For this reason we should ask the Holy Spirit to give us a generous love that begins again and again, and in a certain way renews itself with every passing day. "Called to the act of supernatural love, absolutely gratuitous, the priest should love the Church as Christ has loved her, consecrating to her all his energies and giving himself with pastoral charity in a continuous act of generosity" (*DLM*, n.13). This generosity can show itself in many little things each day: the saying of our Office with attention, notwithstanding personal tiredness and the hectic pace of life; care for those who are sick or in need, particularly for the poorest of our community in whom Christ waits for us in a special way; and especially, continual reverence and faithful adherence to the sacraments, celebrating them in the way the Church wants them to be celebrated. By being loyal to the sacraments, we are being loyal to the One who instituted them and who transmitted them by his Holy Spirit throughout time. The rubrics of the Mass and other sacraments are not ours to change or to modify; as priests we are the instruments of Christ on the altar. We must be faithful to the approved language of the liturgical readings and ceremonies, and not fall into the temptation of political correctness, or the desire to please either those on the right or the left. In other words it is not our Mass, it is His Mass—and we are called to represent Him as his priests.

***

It is a great help to the faithful when they see that we are true to our duties, that we are keeping covenant with the Church, just as we expect them to do. *Lord, may I always deal with holy things in a pious and holy way. According to the ancient adage, sancta sancte tractanda sunt!*

The same applies to the content of our preaching and teaching. We are not at the pulpit or in the classroom to present our own theories about what the Church teaches, or should teach. In union with the Bishop, we are there as representatives of Christ to give our people the Word of God, as preserved and transmitted in His holy Church. That is the only word which is true, the only word which is challenging and life-changing. Of course we should present our homilies and talks in a lively and clear way, using good stories and anecdotes in order to interest and motivate our people. But if we only give people our own experiences and opinions, or, heaven forbid, our doubts and dissent about God and the Church—we should not go up to preach at all. We would be betraying the people of God.

Saint Paul warned Bishop Timothy of this danger in his second letter to him. "O Timothy, guard what has been entrusted to you. Avoid the godless chatter and contradictions of what is falsely called knowledge, for by professing it some have missed the mark as regards the faith" (*I Tim* 6:20-21). Even in those early days there were doubters and dissenters. There were some who proclaimed to have a special "knowledge" (Greek *Gnosis*) that gave them a superior understanding of Christ and his message, and which exempted them from obedience to the Church and her bishops. In the second century one of them, Marcion, even went so far as to form his own Church in Rome and was excommunicated in 144. There are similar trends today. People who call themselves Catholic privately and sometimes publicly dissent from the Church's teachings on human life, the sixth commandment, matrimony, and the authority of the Pope. Just as in the ancient heresies, they think that their ideas are better than Christ's and His authentic Church. At times, in order to be faithful preachers of the Word, we will have to unmask these charlatans and refute their errors.

Again, looking at Saint Paul's correspondence to Timothy, we read what all of us priests must be prepared to do. And I take the liberty to quote him at length, since his words apply so much to our situation today: "I charge thee in the presence of God and of Christ Jesus, who is to judge the living and the dead, and by His appearing and His kingdom: preach the Word, be urgent in season and out of season, convince, rebuke and exhort, be unfailing in patience and in teaching. For the time is coming when people will not endure sound teaching, but, having itching ears, they will accumulate for themselves teachers to suit their own likings and will turn away from listening to the truth and wander into myths. As for you, always be steady, endure suffering, do the work of an evangelist, fulfill your ministry" (II Tim 4:1-5).

***

We too have been given a great treasure—the sacred priesthood in the one true Church founded by Christ, which has the fullness of the means of salvation. Other religions have elements of truth and goodness within them, and we recognize these elements sincerely; but we have to believe that Jesus founded only one Church, which is the means of salvation for all mankind. And it is our deep desire that all men and women can come to the knowledge and participation of that one true Church. "Ut omnes unum sint," that all may be one, was Christ's deepest desire at the Last Supper (cf *Jn* 17:11) and is our desire as well. But we can never draw them into Christ's Body if we betray it by our words or actions, or if we water down the teachings of the Church under the false guise of convincing or converting others. That would be a false ecumenism.

A good part of our fidelity is shown through obedience. This is a most misunderstood word in the contemporary world, since obedience is considered to be something for children only. There is such emphasis on individual freedom that to do the will of someone else can even appear to be demeaning. And yet the redemption of the world came through two persons who obeyed perfectly: Mary of Nazareth and her Son Jesus. They knew that the meaning of their lives was fulfilled precisely in their listening to God's will and carrying it out completely. Our Lady's "Behold the handmaid" and Christ's "Thy will be done" form the model for Christians of all times, especially for us priests. We are men under orders, literally. "Like Christ's, the priest's obedience expresses the will of God that is made manifest to the priest through his legitimate Superiors. This availability must be understood as a true act of personal freedom, the result of a choice continually deepened in the presence of God in prayer" (*DLM*, n.61).

From little things, such as paperwork and diocesan reports, to big things such as new assignments or projects given to us, we need to be generous in our response. In this way God can truly work through us, and we can be instruments of the Holy Spirit on earth.

Fidelity to the Church therefore means fidelity to the structure of authority established by Christ. There is no such thing as the "hierarchical Church" versus the "people's Church," a very deceptive dichotomy introduced after the Second Vatican Council and with absolutely no grounding in that Council. It is clear from the Gospel and the earliest testimonies of Christianity that from the beginning presbyters and other authorities guided the Church, and that Christ bestowed a special power on Peter the first bishop of Rome. In other words, Christ did not found an anarchical Church, but a hierarchical one. In thinking of the Church we must think of the complete body of Christ, which is made up of head, heart, and other members. If that body is disunited from the Head, or vice versa, only death and disunity can follow. For this reason, as priests who transmit Christ's truth and life to the others, we need to be particularly united to the Holy Father and the Bishops. "In reality, the priest, by the very nature of his ministry, is at the service of Christ and the Church. Therefore, he must be disposed to accept all that is justly indicated by his superiors and, in a particular way, if not legitimately impeded, must accept and faithfully fulfill the task entrusted to him by his Ordinary" (*DLM*, n.61).

The Lumen Gentium has an informative section (chapter III) on the bishops and their role in the Church. They are truly vicars of Christ in their dioceses, and they have the fullness of the Sacrament of Orders, especially in the power to teach, to govern, and to sanctify. We priests are called to work very closely, and loyally, with our diocesan Bishop or Prelate in our common mission to sanctify souls. Pope John Paul II connects the role of Bishops and priests with the one priesthood of Christ: "Indeed, between the Bishop and his presbyters there exists a *communio sacramentalis* by virtue of the ministerial or hierarchical priesthood, which is a participation in the one priesthood of Christ.... The presbyters, among them parish priests in particular, are therefore the closest collaborators in the Bishop's ministry" (Post-Synodal Apostolic Exhortation *Pastores Gregis*, October 16, 2003, n.47). Our role as priests therefore is to obey and support them, and to work always in unity with them. In this way the diocese, as a portion of the people of God, can grow in holiness and be a healthy part of the Mystical Body of Christ. We need to have confidence in the Bishop, whoever he is, and keep him well informed about our parish or assignment.

***

Let's try to overcome doubts or suspicions that can arise sometimes, either from ourselves or from others. All of us are poor human beings, including our Ordinary, but the Church continues to be the Mystical Body of Christ, and the Holy Spirit continues to guide it and vivify it. At times we may have to distinguish between what is true obedience to the bishop as the representative of Christ in the diocese, and what are matters of opinion where different solutions are possible. The main point is to remember always Christ's prayer at the Last Supper, *that all may be one*: He wanted this for His apostles and their successors throughout the centuries. And we His priests can assure that unity by our daily prayer for our Bishop—along with our effort to collaborate with him loyally, and to assist him generously in his work of teaching, governing, and sanctifying the faithful.

"The Pope, Bishop of Rome and Peter's successor, is the perpetual and visible source and foundation of the unity both of the bishops and of the whole company of the faithful" (*Lumen Gentium*, n.23). Though bishops represent Christ in their diocese, the Vicar of Christ has full and universal power over the whole Church. As priests we should try to have a particularly close union with the Holy Father; he is *our* Holy Father also. This means, in practice, that we should read his encyclicals, apostolic letters, and other documents carefully, taking them to our prayer and trying to enter more deeply into his mind and intentions. Just as we should do with the writings of our Bishop, we should present our people with the writings of the Holy Father. Perhaps there is a specific idea of his, or certain words that we have seen on the internet or in a Vatican publication, which we know that our people particularly need to hear. Let's take the time to read and study these documents and make them come alive to our people. As good priests, we should also foster love for the Pope as a person, and as a man in need of affection and prayers like everyone else. No matter what is his nationality or personality, he will always be, in the moving words of Saint Catherine of Siena, "il dolce Cristo nella terra (the sweet Christ on earth)." He has a tremendous burden to bear, the governing of a Church with more than a billion members—along with the duty to preserve faithfully the teachings of the Church throughout the centuries, and to assure that as many of the faithful as possible be saved, including others who do not yet belong to the Church. In some ways he is the Shepherd of all mankind. The more we do to help our people, and fellow priests, to listen to and venerate the Pope, the more we are strengthening the Body of Christ on earth.

***

We need to be on guard against an overly provincial view of the Church. Obviously we are members of a specific presbyterate or clergy in a certain territory. Many of us grew up and have families in the same diocese where we now serve. That is good, in a way, because we know the people and the situation well, and therefore can truly serve them. But it could be harmful in another way. We may think that our parish or diocese is the most important thing, and miss the big picture of the universal Church. We could end up thinking and praying for our own people only, without due regard for the Church in other dioceses and countries. In some ways, with the internet and more frequent travel for priests, that narrow view is being overcome. We are instantly aware of what the Pope is saying in Rome, or the needs of the faithful in India, or a situation in Latin America.

All of this should help us to be more universal and truly Roman in our outlook. Let's bring to our prayer the situation of the Church in other dioceses and countries: the shortage of priests, the persecution of the Church in some areas such as India, China, and Africa, the lack of good Catholic formation among many families and children. To use a classical phrase, let us learn to *sentire cum Ecclesia*, that is, to feel the same pain and joys that Catholic men and women feel throughout the world—in union with our brother priests, the bishops, and the Holy Father. This too is part of being faithful to the Body of Christ.

To be truly Catholic is to love all of mankind, and to appreciate the good and valuable contributions of other religions. Unity is a goal given by Christ himself at the Last Supper, and affirmed in different ways by Catholics throughout the centuries, and most recently by the Second Vatican Council. While we are faithful to the Catholic Church, and believe that she is the Church truly founded by Christ with all the means of salvation—we recognize the elements of truth and goodness in other religions. With the Pope and bishops we pray that religious differences be overcome by understanding, prayer, and sincere dialogue. Perhaps some of us have even been engaged in ecumenical encounters of one kind or another. We need to keep praying and working towards the goal when there will be one faith, one Lord, one Baptism. We may have to wait until the Second Coming to see it, but each of us can do his part to make it happen as soon as possible.

As we always do at the end of these reflections, let's have recourse to Mary the Mother of God, *Virgo Fidelis*. It was her faithfulness to her vocation that brought the Church to the world in the Person of her Son. Let's humbly ask her to win the grace of fidelity and obedience for us. Let's also remember that beautiful blue mosaic of Mary installed during the pontificate of Pope John Paul II in Saint Peter's Square; there she presides, holding her Son, over the all the crowds that visit the famous Basilica each day and pray for the Holy Father, whoever he may be. Beneath that colorful mosaic, the only bit of color among all the ancient gray monuments of the Square, are the encouraging words: Mater Ecclesiae, ora pro nobis.

HOLY MASS AND THE EUCHARIST

And when the hour came, He sat at table, and the apostles with Him. And He said to them. "I have earnestly desired to eat this Passover with you before I suffer" (*Lk* 22:14). Before His passion and death, Christ pours forth His soul to those closest to Him. In celebrating the Jewish Passover rite, which commemorated the miraculous freeing of the Hebrews from slavery, Christ himself now becomes the New Passover. He offers himself to his Father as the unblemished Lamb in reparation for sin, and to avert God's wrath. Just as the ancient Passover had united and solidified the people of God into a common faith and heritage, so does Christ's Passover in the Holy Mass unite and solidify all Christians into His Church.

It is our greatest duty and privilege as priests to be able to celebrate the Holy Sacrifice, which perpetuates Christ's love and presence throughout time. By uniting ourselves with His sacrifice, or in the words of Pope Benedict, with "the dynamic of Christ's self-giving," our lives take on a greater meaning, and we become real co-redeemers with Jesus the High Priest at the Last Supper and on Calvary. At every Mass we are also involved in a Trinitarian action which brings life and redemption to the world. Every Mass is the re-actualization of what happened on Golgotha: God the Son offers Himself to God the Father in the love of God the Holy Spirit. And this offering takes place in the most central way at the Consecration, where bread and wine are converted into Christ's Body and Blood, and where Christ renews His sacrifice through His priests—namely you and me.

If we really knew what was happening at every Mass through our poor words and actions, we would surely die. But God is merciful to us; He does not show us the mystery in all of its power but enough for us to adore and give thanks for it. "All good works, taken together, do not equal the sacrifice of the Mass," said Saint John Mary, "since they are human works, while the Mass is the work of God" (Nodet, p.105). Yet despite the marvel and mystery of the Holy Mass, we can easily fall into a superficial, routine view of it. It can become a "job only" for us—something that we're expected to do on Sundays and most weekdays. If we have to binate, or even trinate some days—the Mass could even become burdensome and tiresome for us. Or perhaps we can get caught up by so many details of the celebration that we are more absorbed by them than by the mystery which is taking place. There's the choir, the altar servers, the microphone, the heating and cooling systems, the lectors and extra-ordinary ministers of the Eucharist— I'm sure each of us could add many other distractions that can occur before the Mass. Yet somehow, with the help of the Holy Spirit and our ministerial Archangel, we need to transcend all of these possible distractions in order to focus on the great event about to take place: Christ is coming to the altar, to bring His peace, strength, and salvation to us and our people.

It might be worthwhile to do some mental prayer before we celebrate Mass each day. Let's not simply appear in the sacristy, still half-asleep and unprepared for what we are going to do. Let's not rush in and begin doing things, as if the Mass were a mere routine. By praying ahead of time, by using some of the beautiful prayers from the Church's liturgy—to Our Lady, to Saint Joseph, to the Trinity—we can properly dispose ourselves for God. The individual prayers for vesting with the amice, the alb, the cincture, the stole, and the chasuble are marvelous helps for saying the Mass with true piety: "Impone, Domine, galeam salutis" for the amice; "Dealba me, Domine, et munda cor meum" for the alb; "Praecinge me, Domine , cingulo puritatis" for the cincture; "Redde mihi, Domine, stolam immortalitatis" for the stole; "Domine, qui dixisti jugum meum suave et onus meum leve" for the chasuble.

***

The most important thing is to truly unite ourselves with Christ, who is the principal Priest and Victim at every Eucharist. "If the priest lends to Christ, Most Eternal High Priest, his intelligence, will, voice, and hands so as to offer, through his very ministry, the sacramental sacrifice of redemption to the Father, he should make his own the dispositions of the Master and, like Him, live these gifts for his brothers in the faith" (*DLM* n.48). At Mass we offer the greatest possible praise and adoration to God, as we give Him glory through His Son. This adoration is seen throughout the Mass—in the hymn of praise *Glory to God in the Highest*, in all the Prefaces ending with the Sanctus prayer, in all the Eucharistic prayers culminating in the great doxology "Through Him, and with Him, and in Him…." *Lord, may I never say these prayers of adoration out of routine, or mindlessly; may I understand and love the prayers that I pronounce in each Mass.*

We offer the greatest petition at every Mass. Besides the intention of our stipend, we are certainly free to add many personal petitions, begging God's grace through the sacrifice of His Son for our family and parishioners, for the Church, for the protection of the unborn and other defenseless persons in our society, for the poor, for world peace. These petitions for the living and the dead can be particularly remembered at the commemoration times of the Eucharistic prayers, and at other points of the Mass such as the Prayer of the Faithful.

In union with Christ at the Last Supper and on Calvary we also make atonement for sins at every Mass. He offers equal satisfaction for the sins of all the men and women who ever lived, are living, and will ever live until the end of time. As we lead people in the penitential rite, let us call to mind our sins and the sins of all mankind, remembering that it is Christ's blood that truly reconciles us with God and one another. In His sacred and wounded Heart He makes all to be *at-one* again, which is the etymological origin and primary meaning of *atonement*. We His priests have the privilege of cooperating with Him at every Eucharist in this stupendous work: the reconciliation of all mankind, and indeed the cosmos itself, with His Heavenly Father.

Finally at every Holy Mass we also give thanks, which is the primary meaning of the word Eucharist in Greek. We give thanks to the Father for his grace and forgiveness, for the incalculable gift of His Son's Body and Blood, for making the Church one and united in this sacrament, calling us together in this community banquet. The Prefaces of every Mass highlight our attitude of thanksgiving—"It is right to give Him thanks and praise"—which then extends to the various petitions and commemorations of the Eucharistic Prayer and culminates in the Consecration. Just as He did at the Last Supper and on Calvary, Christ is continually giving thanks to His Father, and we are all uniting ourselves with Him.

***

For the holy priest, the Mass is not over in an hour or half-hour. It should be continued in some form throughout the day, since it is the power source of the Church's life, and as we have said often before, inserts us into the "dynamic of Christ's self-giving." The bread that becomes the bread of life, as we pray at the presentation of gifts, are the phone calls, the appointments, the meetings, the joys or disappointments of our entire day. All of them are on the paten at the Mass; all of them, in some way, become the Body of Christ during the day. And that small bit of water, added to the wine and absorbed later into the rich Blood of Christ, is our daily prayer and work united with the depth of Christ's sacrifice. All the sacraments that we perform, and the work that we do each day, thus become transformed through the Mass and its continuation.

"In a society ever more sensitive to communication through signs and images, the priest must pay adequate attention to all of that which can enhance the decorum and sacredness of the Eucharistic celebration" (*DLM*, n.49). The Liturgy, especially the Holy Eucharist, is far more than an external ceremony. It is the "summit and source" of the Church's life, to use the famous words of Vatican II's *Sacrosanctum Concilium* (n.10). For this reason, since real love and devotion are shown in little things as well as big things, we priests must take care that our liturgies are done correctly, and as far as possible, beautifully. The altar linens, the corporals and veils should be very clean, without a spot of dirt or dust. Our vestments should be clean and well appointed, even splendid to see. The altar and sanctuary areas should also be spotless, with the floors carefully waxed or polished as the case may be.

And of course, in a place of beauty and prominence, the tabernacle should be placed, which is the dwelling place of God Himself. Whether your tabernacle is of classical or more contemporary design, it must be an object that attracts and sustains the devotion of your people—with the vigil candle of course always burning. It may help to have flowers surrounding it, thus highlighting our love and affection for the Lord within. A beautiful image of Christ or His Mother could be placed nearby, to the side or back of the tabernacle, in order to nourish the imagination and prayer of your faithful. And of course, there need to be dignified chairs or pews where people may kneel or sit in order to speak and pray more personally to the Lord in His Real Presence. "Love is repaid by love" a great mystic once said, and certainly your Church and sanctuary should reflect your love for the Eucharist and its surroundings.

But it is not only the external surroundings. Your devotion and love in saying the Mass will certainly give glory to God, but it can also convert your people. That certainly was the experience of the Holy Curé of Ars, who was able to convert atheists and agnostics simply by the depth and fervor of his words at the Eucharist. The way we genuflect, the way we speak (clearly, and without rushing), the way we fold our hands, the sacred silences mandated by the *GIRM* and other recent directives from the Holy See will do great good for your people, and for yourself. The rubrics themselves should be followed carefully; we have no right to interpose our own words or thoughts onto the liturgical texts approved by the Church, including the approved translations for the readings.

Priests can do great harm by changing the words of these texts in order to please certain people, or by falling into a false political correctness with the use of inclusive language. "Those who improperly celebrate the Mass reveal a weakness in their faith and fail to educate the others in the faith" (*DLM*, n.49). "The priest should also follow the rite established in the liturgical books approved by the competent authority, without adding, removing, or changing anything" (*DLM*, n.52). The singing and sacred music are meant to give true glory to God; it should be the kind of music that uplifts and encourages people, without cheapening it to a mundane or worldly level. And of course, it usually falls to the pastor to enforce these necessary indications which the Church has given. It is not dictatorial or authoritarian to insist on dignified music whether the lyrics be in Latin, English, or other languages.

To live the above indications will not make the Mass mechanical or legalistic. On the contrary, it will allow the Holy Spirit to enter your life and that of the faithful. By obeying the indications of the Church, people's lives will be truly edified and uplifted, and above all, real glory will be given to God.

***

The Liturgy of the Word is the first part of the Mass, and formed part of the Eucharistic celebration in the earliest centuries of Christianity. The Sacred Texts should be read with expression and piety, and our homily or sermon must apply those texts to our people in an effective way. As mentioned before, Pope John Paul II once told American priests that they should preach the Gospel with a <u>dynamic fidelity</u>. This means that they should not only be true to the Church's authentic teachings, which are really the teachings of Christ and His Spirit throughout the centuries, but should also present these to the people in a relevant and moving way.

Many expert preachers say that it is good to prepare our homilies or talks a few days beforehand, by reading and praying about the particular text we will be commenting, by thinking of stories or anecdotes that will enliven it, by thinking of ways that the text can be applied to daily life. For instance the text about the blind man from Jericho, Bartimaeus, has excellent practical applications (cf *Mk* 10:46-52). After putting our listeners into the scene, we can illustrate the faith of Bartimaeus, who kept shouting for Christ despite the crowds and despite some who were trying to silence him. Sometimes the world or public opinion—even political correctness—will try to silence us so that we don't speak of God or lead a moral life. In those circumstances we should cry all the louder, as Bartimaeus did, that Christ is truly the Savior of the world. At other times we must humbly ask Christ to give us the light of His truth by saying, "Lord, may I see" as Bartimaeus did. If we preach this way at Holy Mass, we can make Scripture truly come alive for our people, while always affirming the saving truth preserved in the Church's Magisterium.

Devotion to the Holy Eucharist of course does not end with the Sacrifice of the Mass. There are many other traditions and devotions in the Catholic Church, developed over the centuries through the action of the Holy Spirit, which perpetuate the faithful's love and unity with the Blessed Sacrament. "The Church and the world have a great need for Eucharistic worship. Jesus awaits us in this sacrament of love. Let us not refuse the time to go to meet Him in adoration, in contemplation full of faith, and open to making amends for the serious offenses and crimes of the world. Let our adoration never cease" (Pope John Paul II, *Dominicae Cenae*, p. 3). We can do a lot as priests to promote devotion to the Blessed Eucharist. Certainly one way is to offer Exposition of the Blessed Sacrament frequently at the parish, which should include a period for silent adoration and proclamation of the Word according to the approved rite. By offering the opportunity to the faithful to spend time before Christ, we are strengthening their faith, and helping them to connect their lives with His sacrifice. As Pope John Paul II taught, it is also the opportunity to make atonement for sins, our own and those of the whole world, since the Eucharist inserts us into the Sacred and Atoning Heart of Christ.

***

Impelled by the Holy Spirit working through the lay faithful, there has been a tremendous burgeoning of adoration for Jesus in the Sacred Host throughout the United States. Many parishes now have perpetual adoration chapels, often small rooms tastefully decorated with flowers and with books of meditation available. These chapels have provided a real spiritual re-awakening in the lives of countless Catholics, as they volunteer to pray with loving vigilance before the Blessed Sacrament throughout the day and night, in one hour shifts and more. It has surely been a source of vocations for the Church, as we see a direct proportion between the rise of seminary enrollments with the rise of Eucharistic adoration in this country. It is obvious that the Lord in the Blessed Sacrament is calling many to His harvest.

Our own example is very important in this area. It is most edifying and enlightening for people to see their priest adoring the Blessed Sacrament, doing prayer before it, or while reading his Breviary. It helps them to remember the purpose of their own lives as faithful members of the Mystical Body of Christ, and to unite their souls more with their priest. Of course, to pray before the Blessed Sacrament is also most enlightening and strengthening for our own souls as priests. In spending time in devotion and prayer before the Blessed Sacrament, either in the tabernacle or exposed in the monstrance, we ourselves draw closer to Christ the High Priest who waits for us in the Eucharist, and desires to draw us closer to himself. *Lord, may I not miss this great opportunity that I have, living so close to your Real Presence each day. I should yearn to be with you more in order to converse with you, and be strengthened by you. It is also my opportunity to share my joys and sorrows with you, even the foolish imaginings of my mind and heart, or things that trouble me. Lord, I want to take advantage always of your powerful invitation to your apostles—"Abide in me" (Jn 15:4). There I will be secure, there my priesthood will find its fulfillment.*

HOLY PURITY AND CELIBACY

The Sermon on the Mount has often been called the *blueprint* of the Christian life—for in few words Christ proclaims the basic virtues and dispositions needed to follow Him. Giving mercy, living detached from material things, bringing peace to others, having purity of heart are all intrinsic to his calling. The sixth beatitude, purity of heart, has a special resonance and importance in a priest's life, since it will assure his faithful living of celibacy and dedication within the Church.

The original Greek word used for purity (*kathreis*) means something that has no contaminant—very similar to our own use of the term pure water or pure gold. All Christians of course are called to have a clean heart according to their state in life, single or married, but a priest's heart must be particularly clean, without complication or contaminant; he is called to be completely dedicated to Christ and His Bride, the Church. Actually the word "heart" (Hebrew: leb) in Scripture not only applies to the vital organ that pumps the blood but also to the center of one's affections. The heart, in a word, is what makes us tick, what we really *want in life.*

What should we really want as priests? The answer should be clear to us: what we really want is to love Christ above all things and the Catholic Church. To this inseparable Love we have dedicated our lives. We could have chosen to have a wife and children, but we freely renounced that right for something higher and greater. Celibacy is not something that depends on our will only; it is a gift of God (cf. *Mt* 19:11) that allows us to receive a hundredfold and life everlasting. Christ the High Priest set the standard of our dedication as His apostles when He said: "Where your treasure is, there your heart will be also" *Mt* 6:21). What makes us tick should be the treasure of prayer, the sacraments, especially the Holy Eucharist, the good of souls, the authentic teachings of the Church, and our brother priests that we love and support. In receiving the celibate priesthood, we have truly found the "pearl of great price" (*Mt* 13:46), to use the words of the Gospel parable and the expression of Pope Pius XII in his famous 1943 encyclical on virginity.

Lord, may I always give thanks for this great gift, that makes my poor life similar to yours and that of your holy mother! May I always be true to that gift, as the first priests and apostles were, despite my own weakness and the temptations of the world!

Throughout Church history, from the time of Christ and the apostles, celibacy has been the special gift of those completely dedicated to God—whether they be among the lay faithful, ordained clergy, or religious. There is strong evidence that the first bishops and priests either lived celibacy as single individuals, or, if they were married, lived complete continence within Matrimony, with the permission of their wives—as a way to pray more fervently and to serve Christ and the Church more directly. It is true that there was an ecclesiastical law early in the fourth century that mandated celibacy for priests, but the tradition and practice of clerical celibacy certainly go back to the time of Christ and His first apostles (See S.Heid, *Celibacy in the Early Church*, Ignatius Press, San Francisco, 2000). In other words, priestly celibacy was not a man-made law; it originated with the God-Man Himself, who communicated it to His followers.

***

In the contemporary world, chastity is often presented as something negative; it is equated with mere abstinence from sexual experience, or even with a kind of unnatural repression of instincts. But this view completely distorts the purpose and beauty of this great virtue, and especially that of celibacy. "We belong to God completely, soul and body, flesh and bones, all our senses and faculties. Ask Him, confidently: Jesus, guard our hearts! Make them big and strong and tender, hearts that are affectionate and refined, overflowing with love for you and ready to serve all mankind" (St.Josemaria Escrivá, *Friends of God*, n. 177). Though his homily was addressed to everyone, certainly

Saint Josemaria's words in a special way apply to us priests. Chastity, particularly priestly celibacy, is one of the most affirmative and positive realities in this life. It leads to the greatest Love, with a depth and youthfulness that fills both mind and soul with the life of God Himself. It allows us to contemplate and see God more clearly even in this life, as He works in our souls, in others, and in history through His providence. *Blessed are the pure of heart, for they shall see God* (Mt 5:8) really has an exact practical meaning.

Though at times it involves self-renunciation and sacrifice—at times even heroic sacrifice—celibate love for God and his kingdom gives us a hundredfold in this life, and the next. The priest who really has God as his Father, Mary as his Mother, and Christ as his Brother, also has the entire human race as his family. He experiences a joy and spiritual paternity far greater than human fatherhood or family ties. "For he who leaves wives and children and lands for my sake will receive a hundredfold and life everlasting" (*Lk* 18:29). This is the language of victory, not of humiliation or defeat.

Certainly our hearts were made to love and to be loved. A priest is not like a bachelor who has never found a love for his life. The truth is that the priest, or any other person who chooses a life of celibacy for God, has won the lottery of God's love and favor. As a result his mind and heart should be filled with the things of God, the Church, and others. These are truly his treasures. We need to fall in love, above all, with Christ in the Holy Eucharist: He is our King, our Physician, our Shepherd, our greatest Friend. Devotion to Jesus' Most Sacred Heart is most helpful for all priests: for in this way we share in Christ's own love for God and his people; in this way we can give our aspirations, sufferings, and disappointments to Him; in this way we unite ourselves to His thoughts and desires when we preach, administer the sacraments, and live our daily lives.

To live holy purity well, devotion to Mary Mother of God is also essential. She is truly "the woman of our life"; she is our mother and our sweetheart at the same time. Let's have recourse to her often, not only to praise and admire her beauty, but to ask her for help especially in time of temptation. She is that comforting and delightful presence that all of us need—not only to love others, but to let ourselves be loved by her. The Memorare prayer, the holy rosary, or simply brief aspirations of affection and tenderness during the day are sure segues into her Immaculate Heart. We shall never feel alone if we go to her with confidence, at times like small boys who don't know what to do without their mother's help.

***

Our treasure is also in the Church and her faithful. It is important that we greatly value the sacraments and look on them for what they really are: manifestations of Christ's love throughout the centuries. And we are ministers of that love. We are other Christs as we baptize, absolve, consecrate, witness marriages, and anoint His people. Let's ask the Holy Spirit, who is Love Himself—to give us attention and devotion as we administer the sacraments; they can never become for us a mere routine, or a mechanical function. As we preach, even though we will have to challenge and reprimand people at times, we are other Christs who are loving our people (His people), and giving them God's truth.

Any precious gift needs to be cherished, and guarded. People build fences around their lovely gardens; and in past times surrounded the center of their fortress with armies and high sturdy walls. Though holy purity and celibacy is a most precious gift, it can easily be violated or lost. All of us know the immense damage and scandal that the Church has suffered in recent years from priests who betrayed their trust in matters of chastity. Though the causes of this disaster may be complex and multiple, there is one clear solution: "Priests…must not fail to follow those ascetical norms which are proven by the Church's experience and which are demanded even more in present-day circumstances" (*DLM*, n.60).

Each of us must know himself well. For some priests, the computer and its derivatives will be a big obstacle for purity; he will have to restrict himself to solely a minimum and necessary use of it, install a filter that he cannot break, or use it only in a public area where others can see him. Pornography has destroyed many marriages, and has deeply hurt the life and dedication of many priests. The same need for caution can apply to TV programs and movies. There is nothing wrong with rest and entertainment—we all need a certain degree of it—but many newspapers and movies give no real information or entertainment, but only produce a chain of bad ideas and images in our minds.

Of course prudence in dealing with women is essential. The grace of ordination does not take away lust or concupiscence, though it does give us the ability to live celibacy if we are willing to struggle whenever needed and use common sense. Of course we are called to love all the faithful, including women, who are our dear sisters in Christ. But at the same time we have to exercise a special restraint and modesty in our dealings with them. As a caution, when we have to speak with a woman privately, it is better to do so in a room that is more open with other people nearby, or that has glass windows so that others can see us from outside. In this way we will not be alone with a woman in a closed room. This is not a prudish or puritanical measure but a simple precaution based on common sense and unfortunately, upon some very sad experiences of priests with women in the past.

The same good caution and modesty applies to greeting women. Even if done in the open, it is not a good practice for priests to kiss and hug women, with the exception of course of close relatives. Such behavior, even if it seems innocent, can give the wrong signal to both the woman and the priest....let alone be a scandal for some of the faithful. If a priest wants to show regard or esteem for a woman, a warm smile, a friendly bow, or perhaps a handshake should be sufficient.

***

As men in love, with a mission to serve God and his Church, we cannot sell our heritage for a foolish or sinful attachment. This good sense applies to modesty in speech and dress. A priest must be very careful in speaking of sexual matters or situations. It is true that he must address certain issues from the pulpit, but even then he must concentrate simply on the moral law and the Church's teachings, using refined but clear language. In private conversations it is better that he be silent and pray, though he may know many things about others through his pastoral work. And of course, when it comes to matters of Confession, there must be a total and absolute silence.

Related to purity is the cardinal virtue of temperance. It is that virtue by which we moderate our lower impulses and desires in order to obtain the true good, which in our case is the imitation of Christ the man and priest. All of us know, by theological study and by experience, that our sense appetites are disordered because of Original Sin. The desire for pleasure and material things can easily steer us from the path of virtue. It can lead to either mortal or venial sin, and in the worst case, to betrayal of our priestly consecration.

But with the virtue of temperance, we know how to say no to these cravings and disordered desires, in order to say yes to Christ. Saint Josemaria put it clearly when he wrote, "Temperance is self-mastery. Not everything we experience in our bodies and souls should be given free rein.....It is easier to let ourselves be carried away by so-called natural impulses; but this road ends up in sadness and isolation in our own misery" (*Friends of God*, n.84). The fact that vices like overeating or drinking are common in our society, and even in the lives of fellow priests, does not justify intemperance. It does not take a great moral theologian to realize that "Everyone is doing it" is not a valid argument to justify a sin. There is something discordant and jarring in a fat self-indulgent priest; in a certain way he is undercutting his own ministry and credibility by being so.

The good discipline and restraint of temperance will greatly enhance our happiness and effectiveness as priests. We can think more clearly because we are not addicted to food, drink, or a computer. We will be able to appraise situations more objectively, speak more calmly, and really help people who have problems. We can pray better as well. The great mystical writers describe the stages of the spiritual life as purgative, illuminative, and unitive. To proceed beyond the purgative stage we must live temperance well. If we have a habit of sin or over-indulgence in something, our prayer will be impeded. Though of course we can always pray—if for nothing else, for delivery from our attachment—we will not be able to advance in our love and dialogue with God because we are held back by something, even if it be as subtle as a thread.

***

In order to grow closer to God it is helpful to have some voluntary sacrifices or mortifications each day, even in legitimate things. Certainly it is not a sin or lack of temperance to have a glass of beer, but it is an excellent sacrifice to have a glass of water or juice instead; such a sacrifice can strengthen us to resist temptation to over-drinking on other occasions. It is not a sin to eat a sweet roll if we like, as long as we are not on a sugar-free diet or something similar—but it is an excellent sacrifice to have a piece of bread or fruit instead. Such practices are not Manichean or unnatural. We don't hate the body and its appetites (or more accurately, the appetites of our soul through our bodily senses), but we do recognize the need for generous mortification and self-denial—which will make us stronger for Christ and his service, and increase the quality of our prayer.

The need for temperance and balance also applies to speech. We need not, at times should not, say the first thing that comes to our mind. It can often be misunderstood, and can wound people. We all know of people, whole families that have left the Church because of a rude or imprudent thing said by a priest. That reaction may not seem fair to us, but it's a fact. It is better to wait and pray, and say things in a calmer more reflective way. The same thing applies to gossip or loquaciousness. Priests cannot be "tale-bearers" or spend their time speaking of the faults of others, including other priests or the bishop. The ancient adage states, "If you cannot praise, say nothing." There is great wisdom in that advice, though it may mean that we need to be silent many times.

People will also have a hard time trusting us with their problems and confidential situations, if they know that we cannot control our tongue. The same good discipline applies to moods of anger or negativity. Priests cannot afford to give themselves the luxury of a bad mood. They must be pleasant, affable, and easy to deal with. People should feel free to approach them and speak with them. But if we give into sarcasm or wounding remarks, our pastoral work would suffer greatly. Instead of drawing persons closer to us, and eventually to Christ Himself, we would repel them.

There is also a good balance in our use of the imagination and intellect. Our imagination can be a helpful faculty for praying, preaching, and writing—but it can also be a disordered source of distraction and worry. Many times we will have to say no to our imagination or curiosity in a gentle but consistent way—so that we can work and pray better. We need to discipline the desire for escape or fun, in order to give ourselves more completely to our work. There certainly is a time for rest and entertainment—it should be part of our schedule—but a constant desire to escape, either by sports, reading, TV, or other distractions can only hinder us from the work we must do as priests. A disordered imagination can also be the source of many temptations, especially against purity and even hope.

Can there be too much desire for knowledge or learning? The answer has to be yes, if such knowledge takes us away from our duties as Christ's priests. For instance, a priest who reads books continually, even good theology books, but who does not pray his Office or take care of his people, is committing a sin of intellectual intemperance. Of course we have to read and study things all of our life to be effective preachers and spiritual directors, but we must not forget that "scientia inflat": knowledge puffs up if it takes us away from true charity. Many times we will have to curtail our study or desire to read if our people need our assistance. At the same time, we should learn how to make a good schedule for ourselves. Paradoxically, it's intemperate to say yes to every request of individuals if this takes us away from prayer and the formation we need to be dedicated priests doing Christ's work.

Saint Paul writes of himself and the first Christians: "For we are the fragrance of Christ for God, alike as regards those who are saved and those who are lost" (*II Cor* 2:15). Because we are priests, like it or not, people will notice us more. They will see how much wine we take at social gatherings; they will hear the words we choose, and when we desire to speak, and when we remain silent; they will certainly notice the kind of car we drive, and perhaps even know where we go on vacation or how our rectory is furnished. If we are intemperate, if we spend money foolishly and have many possessions and attachments it will hurt their faith, even though we don't mean it to do so. But if we are temperate and live a generous spirit of self-denial in our life, we will be that good aroma and fragrance of Christ for others, of which Saint Paul speaks (cf *II Cor* 2:15).

And we can also attract more men, either younger or older, to consider following our path as priests. What a great gift we give to the Church if we truly say no to ourselves by a life of temperance and restraint….in order to give ourselves sincerely to God and others.

SHARING CHRIST'S CHALLENGE OF HOLINESS

At one point in His public ministry, as if to summarize what He had previously stated, our Savior told a large group of people:...*be perfect as your heavenly father is perfect* (*Mt* 5: 48). He was not speaking simply to His apostles or closer disciples, but to people of all ages and backgrounds...men and women, rich and poor, educated and uneducated. They were all to aspire to perfection and holiness. This challenge was well understood and lived by the earliest generations in the Church (we can see this clearly in the writings of the apostles and some of the early Christian Fathers). Saint Paul and others actually address the Christians in various cities as "saints" and urge them to imitate the life of Christ personally. Saint Peter in his second letter calls them "a royal priesthood, a holy nation, God's own people, that you may declare the wonderful deeds of Him who called you out of darkness into His marvelous light" (*I Peter* 2:9).

In later centuries, for some reason, the call to holiness and the fullness of God's love was considered more proper to the religious state, to those who left the world and took special vows; the original Gospel call to holiness for all the faithful was either forgotten or not emphasized. In the twentieth century this call was re-presented to the Church and world through the pioneer work of Saint Josemaría Escrivá, the Founder of Opus Dei. "Don't let your life be sterile; blaze a trail...Shine forth with the light of your faith and of your love" (*Way* #1). This point and many others in his writings have definite resonance with the way the early Christians lived their faith, and certainly with the words of the Master Himself when He tells his followers, "You are the light of the world; you are the salt of the earth" (*Mt* 5:13.14).

There is no reason to think that in the 21st century God has ceased calling His people to be saints. Despite the ravages of secularism and relativism in modern society, His grace continues to work in people's souls, moving them to dedicate their lives to Himself and to others. The Catholic Church is still the leaven working in the world, preparing mankind to discover Christ when He comes, and encouraging and enlightening people to be true to God's will. As priests we have the mission to remind people of "who they are," and to give them the means to become holy and to help others, beginning with their families, to become holy. We can't allow the lay faithful to slip into a comfortable, mediocre view of themselves or their lives.

Of course the best and greatest way to help the lay faithful to become saints is through the sacraments. As said often in this little book, a priest who says Mass with attention and devotion is helping thousands of souls. Since the source of holiness is Christ and His burning love—the more priests connects people with Christ's life and Eucharistic sacrifice, the holier they will become. This was the great secret of the Curé of Ars' life, and is the secret of every priest's life. Besides the Mass, his ministry at the Confessional is also crucial, since this is the means to bring back souls to Christ's Sacred Heart and communion with His Church, as well as being an immense source of grace for people's daily struggle. Indeed all the sacraments, well administered and performed with care, are the chief sources of grace for the lay faithful: Baptism, which forgives Original Sin, infuses sanctifying grace, imprints an indelible character on their souls, and initiates them into the Church; Matrimony, which unites a man and a woman with Christ and His Church, and gives them the grace to sanctify their relationship, as well as raise and educate the children in the Faith; Confirmation, which strengthens them for the battle for truth and charity in the world, and which perfects baptismal grace; Anointing, which prepares the soul for eternal life, and often gives the grace of physical healing.

***

By devoting himself assiduously to the sacraments, and by trying to administer them better each time, a priest is truly sanctifying the people entrusted to him: young and old, rich and poor, healthy and sick. He should consider particularly that the Holy Mass and Eucharist will fortify them with the Body and Blood of Christ. By offering their lives in union with Jesus on the altar, they can sanctify all of their daily tasks. We could even state that each of them will be saying his or her own *24-hour* Mass by continuing in the presence of God all day long. By receiving the Eucharist regularly, and with a strong life of prayer, priests can become true contemplatives without the need to enter a convent or a monastery. "I talk about the interior life of ordinary Christians who habitually find themselves in the hubbub of the city, in the light of day, in the street, at work, with their families or simply relaxing; they are centered on Jesus all day long. And what is this except a life of continuous prayer?" (Saint Josemaria, *Christ is Passing By*, n.8).

The good priest does not forget the importance of challenging his people to become saints. This he can do most effectively through his preaching and advice in the Confessional and spiritual direction. While being compassionate with human weaknesses always—and certainly aware of his own faults—he should keep in mind the most important goal for his people. They should be leading a life of intense prayer, they should be avoiding anything that would offend God, they should have a great charity towards one another, they should be the Lord's apostles in the world, giving witness to his Truth and Love, and bringing many into His Church. They too need retreats and spiritual exercises that will keep them close to God. They too need to examine their consciences regularly, as we priests must also do, to make sure that they are not giving into egotism, avarice, anger, or lust.

It's quite possible for us to think subconsciously, even though we would never articulate it as such, that lay people are called to a lower grade of holiness, and cannot be challenged very much. We may think that marriage for instance cannot really be sanctified, since it is only a natural institution, existing mostly for the satisfaction of instinct and the procreation of children. Or we can identify Matrimony simply with the liturgical service that we must conduct in Church. The truth is that it is a sacrament, the *magnum sacramentum*, that reflects Christ's own love for His Church (see Eph.5), and that husband and wife are called to help each other to obtain eternal life, and to form their children to obtain heaven also. Through the daily trials and effort to raise a family together, husband and wife can become truly great saints if they are faithful to God's teaching on marital chastity and fidelity, and if they truly sacrifice themselves for one another.

The same thing applies to their life of prayer and their work. There is no reason for us to think that "it's enough that they get to Mass on Sundays and Holy Days." That's minimalist thinking. Rather, we have to affirm that lay people can live a contemplative life and be in contact with God all day long. Saint John Chrysostom, one of the Fathers of the Church, wrote these words back in the fourth century: "A woman busy in her kitchen or sewing some cloth can always lift her thoughts to heaven and invoke the Lord with fervor. One who goes to the market or travels alone can easily pray attentively. Another in his wine cellar, busy sewing wineskins, is free to raise his heart to the Master....No place is lacking in decorum for God" (4th *Homily on Anna, Mother of the Prophet Samuel*, 6) By offering their work generously, therefore, men and women living in society can turn their entire day into a prayer for Christ.

***

We can also encourage the lay faithful to find time for more personal dialogue with God each day—whether at Church or at the Adoration Chapel, or simply by saying aspirations on the street. Devotion to Mary is always of great assistance for everyone in the Church, especially the recitation of the rosary, either alone or with others. If they are to be the "light of the world" they certainly must know their faith well, and how to defend it and propagate it. For this reason let's urge them to read worthwhile books written by the saints and sound theologians, or to consult good Catholic websites. By absorbing and interiorizing these spiritual ideas they can begin to transform businesses and secular professions into places of grace and real service for society. In other words, as priests we need to encourage and motivate the lay faithful to become saints. Since they're in the middle of the world, they can reach and influence many more people than we can—including atheists, agnostics, and fallen away Catholics. If they are men and women of prayer and sound ideas, they can bring back myriad souls to Christ.

At the same time that we encourage and challenge the lay faithful, let's always be respectful of their freedom. They too are children of God, they too must make their own decisions and commitments, including how to conduct their spiritual life. "For all who are led by the Spirit of God are sons of God. For you did not receive the spirit of slavery to fall back into fear, but you have received the spirit of sonship" (*Rom* 8:14-15). In dealing with our brothers and sisters in the laity, let's try to avoid any kind of clericalism. The desire to control the laity, or to have them do things *our way* is not healthy. We are clerics, they are not. To think of the laity only in relation to the parish and its programs is very limiting; most of their lives will be spent with their families, friends, at work or travel, and other activities. As priests we do not want them to serve us, but rather we should serve them: we respect their individuality and their own paths to holiness. While always following the basic teachings of the Church in faith and morals, they should feel free to do as they wish in their family life, work, and prayers. As a matter of fact being free is an essential characteristic of being a Christian, and a son and daughter of God. For freedom Christ has set us free, writes Saint Paul. "Stand fast therefore, and do not submit again to the yoke of slavery" (*Gal* 5:1).

Let's be very careful of any desire to control or manipulate the lay faithful, or to use our priestly position as an excuse to dictate the way they should live their lives. It is true that at ordination we received the three offices of ruling, teaching, and sanctifying—but we must be careful to restrict these to our spiritual duties as priests and not interfere in the free terrain of the lay faithful. For instance we cannot be like the priest who considers that laypeople can only be good Catholics by participating in ecclesiastical activities, or *his* activities; this would be clericalism. Or we cannot be like the priest who doesn't appreciate initiatives of the lay faithful and other movements in the Church that are international, or that come from outside of his diocese…as if the Holy Spirit were limited to his territory only! Or like a priest who doesn't respect the right of association of the lay faithful, and their freedom and responsibility in temporal affairs, thinking that everything they do at work or with their friends must somehow be an ecclesiastical activity, or some kind of ministry.

Most lay faithful do not have or need "ministries." They're simply good fathers and mothers, students, or conscientious workers who communicate Christ's message to those around them in a natural and personal way. Let's give thanks for that: it is the action of the leaven in the world of which Our Lord Himself speaks (cf *Mt* 13:33). We don't want to clericalize the laity, but we do want them to use the priestly soul given to them in Baptism: that is, the power to act as other Christs in the world, and to direct, teach, and sanctify those around them, including their families and companions at work.

Let's think of the lay faithful, therefore, as Christ and the apostles did. They too are called to give themselves to God in their daily life. When Saint Peter reminds them that *they are a holy people, and a royal priesthood* (*I Peter* 2:9), it means that through Baptism they share in the three-fold ministry of Christ as King, Teacher, and Sanctifier. Therefore they are called to transform and structure society in accord with the moral law and God's grace. They are called to change and renew the practice of medicine, science, law, the manual trades and arts, sports and entertainment, and most especially, the home. They are called to be witnesses of the Church's truth, especially in such crucial areas today as the protection of human life, ethics in business, sexual morality, the fostering of family life, and care for the poor and needy. They must teach their children and many others about the truth and love of God. Finally, they must try to sanctify the society that they live in, so that through their work, prayers, and sacrifices they can bring grace into the world, as the Master did through his ordinary life and his death on the cross. It is not exaggerated to say that the ordinary faithful are "co-redeemers" with Him, for they can bring hope and salvation to others by connecting their lives with Christ in His daily work and on the cross.

To give the lay faithful these high goals of prayer, sacrifice, and apostolate is our work as priests. The Church grew and will always go forward when priests and the lay faithful work in cooperation with each another. Even though the priesthood of ordained ministers differs from the common priesthood "essentially, not only in degree" (Vatican II, *Lumen Gentium*, n.10), both priesthoods work together. We ordained priests provide the sacraments and spiritual direction to the lay faithful so that they can truly become saints, and bring others to the Church as well. The lay faithful assist us by their prayers and sacrifice, by preparing future priests in the warmth of their homes, and by bringing us their family and friends for the sacraments and spiritual guidance.

***

In addition to forming the lay faithful to accomplish their baptismal mission, we as ministers of Christ should have a preferential love for the poor. We must often hear Christ's words to us, "As you did it for one of these the least of my brethren, you did it to me" (*Mt* 25:40). The poor could be literally someone without food or shelter, a family that's struggling to pay their debts, a parishioner who is sick, an abandoned man or woman in a nursing facility who is never visited by anyone, or perhaps a wealthy man or woman who is lonely and without real friendship or purpose in their lives. Whatever the circumstance, we as ministers of Christ's Sacred Heart have a call to help them. We need to be generous in making visits to the hospital when one of our people needs the sacraments. We will have to move out of our "comfort zone," so to speak, if a person needs to be anointed, or a poor person needs to be consoled. One of the great spiritual works of mercy we can do is simply to teach someone who is ignorant of God and His Catholic Church.

To do all of the above, we will need the help of God's grace of course, which gives us the ability to not think of ourselves. Remembering the laity's call to holiness, we should preach frequently about care for the disadvantaged. Many priests work closely with already established charitable groups in their parish or in the diocese to administer to the poor. Others form groups of faithful to attend to the needs of the sick or the abandoned. Both are excellent ways to help the lay faithful to become saints. In practicing the works of mercy, they are imitating Christ himself. When a father with his children volunteer their time at a soup kitchen, or rehab a damaged home for a needy family, they are truly spreading the love of Christ to others. When a mother and her children volunteer to say the rosary before an abortion clinic, or when they participate in a pro-life event, or, even better, when they dissuade a young woman from having an abortion they are doing the greatest corporal work of mercy: *saving a human life.* They may also be doing the greatest spiritual work of mercy possible: saving a soul—that of the young woman who was about to abort her child.

***

As priests we need to pray often to the Holy Spirit for the energy and words to inspire our people to be other Christs, living to the full their call to holiness both in the single or married state. Let's remind them frequently that they too have been chosen by God for a great mission: to give glory to God in all that they do, and to transform society. They are not second-class citizens in the Church but have received the grace to love God above all things, and to be his witness in their daily lives. Their work contributes in some way to the new heaven and the new earth prophesied in the Book of Revelation, for nothing good of human endeavors is ever lost in the eyes of the Creator. God has a plan for each one of these men and women that is both loving and challenging. They are not mere statistics in a heartless universe but sons and daughters especially chosen by God before creation began. Saint Paul put this very expressively in his first chapter to the Ephesians. Though he was speaking to the first Christians, the lay faithful of today should hear him speaking to themselves: "Blessed be the God and Father of our Lord Jesus Christ who has blessed us in Christ with every spiritual blessing in the heavenly places, even as He chose us in Him before the foundation of he world, that we should be holy and blameless before Him" (*Eph* 1:3). Baptized men and women in the Church should therefore try to imitate the thoughts, words, and actions of Christ Himself. They too are created in the image and likeness of God, and will find their fulfillment as persons in the gift of themselves…as Christ gave himself to His Father and to each human person. Theirs is an authentic call from God that includes prayer, work, Christian witness in society, and a preferential love for those who are poor or needy.

Mary of Nazareth could also be called an ordinary member of the lay faithful. As a homemaker with a husband and child, she went about her duties of service to her family and relatives, participated in the social life of the village, and went to the synagogue for her prayers. Later as a Christian she would continue serving as the mother of her Son's people, and living with the family of Saint John. And yet, despite the "ordinariness" of her life she was the greatest saint that ever lived, truly loving God and others in everything that she did. In speaking to the lay faithful, and challenging them to lead holy lives, let's go often to her for her example and intercession, along with her spouse Saint Joseph.

REDEMPTIVE SACRIFICE

The word sacrifice comes from two Latin words, *sacrum facere*, which literally means to make something sacred. In ancient religions people would offer something valuable to God to show their homage, and in offering this object—which could be a material thing, an animal, or even a person—they considered that their sacrifice was a truly sacred action. Even if their ideas were confused about the One God, and some of their practices were cruel or immoral, they had the deep conviction that their gods or deity were worth the pain of giving up something, in order to show honor to them, and to beseech their favor.

For us Christians the greatest sacrifice of course was that of Jesus Christ's voluntary offering of Himself on the cross. Unlike any other sacrifice before it, He Himself was both the Priest and Victim. Through His suffering He paid the greatest homage to God that could ever be paid and obtained the greatest favor that could ever be obtained. There His whole Being, Body and Soul, was made sacred to God as He offered His life for us, though of course as the Son of God He was already sacred to His Father. This is My Body, which will be given up for you; This is My Blood, which will be shed for you. The very words of the Consecration of the Mass are sacrificial. They are the words of a Priest and Victim who is giving everything for us.

We priests, as ministers of Christ, must also be men of sacrifice. If we are to bring grace and hope to the world, we must somehow share in the source of all grace and hope, which is the generous self-offering of Jesus on the cross. Rather than a cause of anxiety or complaint for us, this offering should be a kind of victory for us. Paraphrasing the stirring words of Saint Paul, we affirm this conviction in the liturgy of the Mass of the Lord's Supper every year: "Nos autem oportet gloriari in cruce Domini Nostri Jesu Christi: It's necessary for us to glory in the cross of our Lord Jesus Christ" (Gal.6:14)

In no way does this mean that we should be seeking pain for the sake of pain, or for some kind of egotistic satisfaction. That kind of behavior is really a psychological illness, often called masochism or sadism. Real Christian mortification has a much different root; it is rooted in freedom and the desire to be purified of sin and selfishness. It seeks to connect oneself with the suffering Christ in order to bring hope and salvation to the world. This kind of sacrifice, in union with the Savior's cross, is never a humiliation, but rather a liberation. In the above text the Apostle even connects it with victory.

As Catholics therefore we believe that mankind will not saved by technological advances, political change, a strong military, a bustling economy, or even great works of literature or art. Each of us is saved in only one way: by personal union with the life of the Son of God, and often we will find Him next to, or nailed to His cross.

***

"A sharp pain pierces the soul of Jesus; our Lord falls to the ground exhausted. You and I can say nothing; now we know why the cross of Jesus weighs so much....From the depths of our soul there comes an act of real contrition..." (St. Josemaria, *Way of the Cross*, Third Station, p.38). Contact with the suffering Christ has three main benefits: it purifies us from pride, laziness, sensuality and other obstacles that hurt our soul; it atones for sin, which is one of our central missions as priests; it brings grace and hope to the world. Regarding the first benefit, let's recall Saint Paul's famous words: " Put off your old nature which belongs to your former way of life...and be renewed in the spirit of your minds, and put on the new nature..."(*Eph* 4:22.23). The new man is Christ, the old man is the man of sin and selfishness. As priests we should examine ourselves each day to see if we are struggling against pride. It could be the desire for attention, the comparing of ourselves with others, or simply the ambition to receive ecclesiastical honors. If we're to be men of service, we must always remember

Christ's words: "Whoever would be great among you must be your servant" (*Mt* 20:26)

The struggle against laziness can be made specific in different ways: getting up when we should each day, allowing time for prayer before we say Mass; doing our work punctually, without delay or last minute rushing; volunteering to undertake difficult but worthwhile projects. We also need to confront hard situations at the necessary moment, without running from them. Regarding the disorder of sensuality, we can learn to offer a sacrifice or small act of self-denial for each meal we take: eating more slowly perhaps, taking more of what we don't like, not snacking between meals, fasting on certain days and occasions. Little things like posture while sitting can also be a good sacrifice.

At times interior sacrifices can be the best for making us more Christ-like. That is, not giving into thoughts, memories, or desires that are at best a waste of time. These could take the form of a certain nostalgia for the "good old days" that separates us from our daily tasks and duties, or they could be a kind of escapism into the future: "in ten years we'll have another bishop, the Church will change, the economy will be better, etc." Or perhaps the tendency to run away or not face our work can lead to different kinds of wishful thoughts: "I wish I had a different pastor, I wish I were in a different diocese, I wish I had different classmates, etc...." Finally, there also exists for each of us the danger of self-pity. We can begin to think that no one understands or cares about us, that our work is useless, or that we never get any recognition for the hard work that we are doing. We can even begin to invent tragedies in our mind, in which we are the principal victim. In this regard I remember that humorous quote of Mark Twain in one of his books, when he's speaking about the many hard times that he has had: "Yes, I've been through a thousand terrible things in life, and two of them actually happened."

Mortification of the memory and desires keeps us true to our mission as priests, and helps us to imitate the actions of Christ the Good Shepherd. It also helps us to be more objective and realistic about life. "Your crucifix: As a Christian you should always carry a crucifix with you. Place it on your desk. Kiss it before you go to bed and when you wake up. And when your poor body rebels against your soul, kiss your crucifix!" (*The Way*, n.302).

***

In the same way, let's look for sacrifices that can atone for sin. We adore you, O Christ, and we bless you—for by your holy cross you have redeemed the world. So we often proclaim when we pray the *Way of the Cross*. Christ made up for the sinfulness and disobedience of all men through His voluntary pain on the cross. We too must be co-redeemers. When we hear confessions, let's offer extra reparation for sins like the Holy Curé of Ars. While we don't have to spend long hours on our knees as He did—maybe we can offer a special sacrifice at a meal that day, or recite an extra decade of the rosary on our knees, or offer an hour of work in atonement for the sins that we have heard. The same atoning spirit applies when we read of something in the newspapers, perhaps a scandal or a murder. Rather than just shaking our head sadly, or shrugging our shoulders helplessly at the tragic condition of the world, we could say an act of reparation such as "Father forgive them" or "Jesus have mercy on us." We can do the same if we happen to pass by a hospital or clinic where immoral operations are performed, or a movie theatre showing bad films. Rather than pass by indifferently, let's have recourse to our Lord's most Sacred Heart in order to make atonement for those offenses to God through him.

So many times in our ministry we too shall be a man of sorrows, acquainted with grief (*Is* 53:2), as the Savior was. One sorrow may be in confronting the fact of death so frequently, and having to console the deceased person's relatives with an encouraging word; it may be the frustration of having few people come to confession, despite our preaching and urging; it may be the discouragement of speaking with engaged couples who are living together, and who seem to have little appreciation for the sacrament that they are about to receive. It may simply be a lot of administrative work in the parish, with constant calls and demands on our life. We may even ask ourselves, "Was I ordained to be an office administrator or a fund-raiser?" All these are times for us to grow in love for God, letting Christ's grace purify us from our impatience or pride, and using these circumstances to make atonement for sins: literally, we are putting "at one" the erring world with the God who heals and forgives.

Mortification or sacrifice brings grace and redemption to the world. "For if the grain of wheat does not die, it shall never produce fruit" (*Jn* 12:24). There is great treasure in suffering voluntarily for holy intentions. As priests we have many intentions: the persons for whom we've promised to pray; conversions of individuals back to the Church; marriages which are threatened; big crises that face the nation and the world, such as terrorism, abortion, the undermining of the family. Let's never think that our prayers are insignificant or meaningless. Pope Benedict expressed the depth of hope that comes from suffering with Christ in a powerful way in his second encyclical: "Man is worth so much to God that He Himself became man in order to *suffer with* man in an utterly real way—in flesh and blood—as is revealed to us in the account of Jesus' Passion. Hence in all human suffering we are joined by one who experiences and carries that suffering *with* us; hence *consolatio* is present in all suffering, the consolation of God's compassionate love—and so the star of hope rises" (*Saved in Hope*, n.39).

***

We priests then are in a marvelous position to connect ourselves with the redemptive suffering of Christ, personally and sacramentally, especially through the Holy Sacrifice of the Mass. This is our greatest privilege every day, when we can unite all that we do "through Him, and with Him, and in Him." Along with Confession, Holy Mass purifies us of our sinfulness, as Christ's grace permeates and transforms us. But it is also the way of true atonement and reparation for the sins of the world, along with the ever-fruitful source of grace and hope for those around us.

The lay faithful, through their own prayer and sacrifices, also bring grace and redemption to the world. In this regard I recall the story of a ten year old boy who was diagnosed with bone cancer in the years shortly after World War II. The parish priest of his family would visit him frequently, and pray with him, along with his father and mother. Sometimes he would play checkers with him, and say the rosary, after which the little boy would go to Confession. One day the Holy Spirit inspired the priest to ask the boy if he wanted to do some good with all of his suffering. "You know, Eddy," he said, "there are so many people in Japan who do not know Jesus. We just finished a terrible war with them, and so many of them died. And there are so few Christians among them. Why don't you offer your sufferings and pray for their conversion?" The little boy nodded eagerly and said that he would do it, as if it were a kind of game. The next day after remembering the boy and his family in a special way at Mass, he paid him a visit and asked what kind of night he had. The boy answered: "O Father, I had a terrible night. I couldn't sleep at all, I have this tremendous thirst, and my bones feel like they're on fire. But…" and here he halted a bit and looked at the priest with a little twinkle in his eye, "but I bet a thousand people converted in Japan." The priest laughed a bit with the boy when he heard it, but afterward when he was by himself he began to weep because he knew that somehow he had just been with Christ, and had seen the secret of the world's salvation in that small boy.

If ever we try to run from the effort or sorrows that go with priesthood, if ever we are tempted to complain or water down our dedication, let's have recourse to Mary Mother of Sorrows. "Stabat Mater iuxta crucem" begins that famous hymn used in the *Way of the Cross*. Our Lady does not faint or cry out hysterically on Calvary. She stands there bravely, taking into herself the agony of her Son, uniting herself completely to His pain and to His intentions. She will give us the strength to endure, and to be faithful priests. She will help us to transform our sufferings into her son's saving work on the cross, to mingle our small drop of blood into the ocean of Christ's redemptive love.

CARING FOR OUR BROTHERS IN THE PRIESTHOOD

We've seen before that Christ established the Eucharist, the New Passover, as a result of His sacrificial love. And it was also during that supper that He gave His greatest manifestation of friendship and fraternity to His apostles. He did something shocking and inconceivable to them: He washed their feet. He girded a towel, took a basin of water and went to each one of them—a ritual that many of us also perform on Holy Thursday of each year. It's as if Christ wanted to show His personal and fraternal care towards each one of them before giving them the greatest manifestation of love of all: the Holy Eucharist.

It is no wonder that He chose to conclude His charitable action, after the traitor apostle had left, with the New Commandment (the Mandatum Novum): "A new commandment I give to you, that you love another…by this all men will know that you are My disciples, if you have love for one another" (Jn 14:34.35).

It was this command that distinguished the life of the early Christians particularly, to the complete astonishment of the pagan world. How could men and women from different countries and backgrounds have such concern and love for one another? It seemed absurd to non-believers, but the Christians were only following the Master's command. Though the practice of charity became widespread among His followers, let's remember that He gave that command **first** to His apostles and priests. They were to have a great love and fraternity with one another, which would then be transmitted to all the faithful.

Oh Lord, that makes me think. How is it that I am quite charitable with parishioners or other friends, yet can be so cold and critical of priests? Correct me, Lord. Let me hear that new commandment of the Last Supper always ringing in my ears: love your brothers in the priesthood, as I have loved you in the washing of the feet and in the Eucharist.

The unity that we have with our brother priests is a unity of vocation and inner being. By Holy Orders we have all been configured with Christ the High Priest. This Configuration is something even beyond our own blood relations; it is based upon an indelible priestly character imprinted on our souls. "By virtue of the sacrament of Holy Orders every priest is united to other members of the priesthood by specific bonds of apostolic charity, ministry, and fraternity. He is in fact inserted into the Ordo Presbyterorum constituting that unity which can be defined as a true family in which the ties do not come from flesh nor from blood but from the grace of Holy Orders" (*DLM*, n.25).

***

The first part of charity in any family is to wish people well. Just as we would wish a brother or sister to succeed in what they do, we should wish the same for our brothers in the priesthood. Let's pray that they be successful, for the glory of God and good of souls, in their apostolic assignments. We pray that they be good homilists, that they draw many to Confession, that they give good spiritual direction, that they be a source of consolation and support for the poor and the needy. If they are teachers at a school or the seminary, that they give truly helpful classes…faithful to the Church's Magisterium yet challenging and inspiring for their students.

So much of charity is knowing how to be a real friend. As human beings we have the capacity of being friends of others, and many of us had good friends before becoming priests. But with our brothers in the presbyterate, who share with us a common mission and dedication, our friendship should be more elevated and refined. "The capacity to develop and profoundly live priestly fraternity is a source of serenity and joy in the exercise of the ministry, a decisive support in difficulties and a valuable help in the growth of pastoral charity. Priests must exercise this friendship in a particular way precisely towards those brothers most in need of understanding, help and support" (*DLM*, n.28).

If one of our brothers is sick or particularly burdened in his work, why not volunteer to say a Mass for him or hear confessions? With elderly priests, even though they may not have been in our ordination class, we may wish to visit at times and tell them things that could amuse or entertain them. If we know of any recently ordained priests, or seminarians, we can take them with us—not only to live the unity of the presbyterate but also to encourage and hearten an elderly priest who would be particularly cheered by seeing a younger priest. Of course all of us, through the Communion of Saints, can be praying for deceased priests. The diocesan *ordo* usually has a necrological list of priests by name on one side of the page, with the date and year of their passage into eternity. Let's pray to them and ask for their assistance, since they know our life and struggles very well. And of course, for any deceased priest that may not yet be with God, let's offer generous suffrage for his soul. *What a great act of charity, Lord, for me to remember those who have gone before me. Let no priest remain in Purgatory; may they all enjoy eternal life, and continue to help us here on earth through their intercession.*

***

Above all, of course, we want our brothers to become saints—in this life and the next. The greatest favor we can do for a priest is to give him the encouragement, the prayer, and perhaps the timely correction that he needs to persevere in his vocation...."I have called you friends, for all that I have heard from my Father I have made known to you" (*Jn* 15:15). Good friends share what is good with one another; they enjoy each other's company, and their mutual relationship enriches them both. Christ's words show that the ultimate consequence of friendship is to help someone find God and eternal life. And that is precisely the greatest good that we can offer to our brothers in the priesthood, and hope that they will do the same for us. Going back to John 15, we see that Christ continues to speak with his apostles in a most personal and sincere way: "You did not choose me, but I chose you and appointed you that you should go and bear fruit and that your fruit should abide…" (*Jn* 15: 16). Though in our own eyes it might seem that *we* chose our vocation to become priests, in reality it was He who chose us…and other priests as well. Now we must bear fruit, and help our brothers to do so.

Let's offer our prayers each day for the priests of our diocese or community, not only for those that are happy and doing well, but especially for those who need special care. Perhaps we know of one or two who seem to be drifting from their dedication. It's not hard to see the signs: if he is continually critical about his situation, if he expresses doubts about the Church's teaching in key areas, if he doesn't say the Breviary or other prayers, if he goes on vacation to places that are very worldly and can easily become occasions of sin. Let's particularly pray for a priest in this situation. If we know him well enough, we can speak with him face to face about our concerns, after examining our conscience to make sure that we don't have the same fault, and if we do, that we are struggling against it. If he doesn't listen to us, and if the matter is particularly grave, we can speak of it to another priest friend who can also bring it up with him, or to one of the superiors of the diocese who can help him.

We all remember, very painfully, the great harm that was done to the Church in this country recently by the lack of guidance and good spiritual direction for priests who had dangerous habits and tendencies, especially in dealing with children and minors. In the same vein we cannot just "look the other way" if we know of serious situations such as active homosexuality, alcoholism, addiction to pornography, or sinful attachment to a woman. Real charity demands in these circumstances that we speak clearly and act in time—for the good of our brother, and for the good of others in the Church.

***

Love has keen eyes. In some way we must cultivate the heart of a father and a mother with our fellow priests. For instance, we may notice some who seem tired and exhausted by their jobs. Perhaps we could suggest an outing to them—and take a walk in the country with them, go bike riding, see a good movie, or play a sport. Oftentimes, like everyone else, priests simply need to relieve their minds, and talk about things that are frustrating them. Though we may not be their confessors or spiritual directors, we can certainly share our own experiences in order to help them. Since we face many of the same issues and frustrations in our own life, our encouragement can be of value to them. We may even be able to direct them to a good confessor or spiritual guide who will be of service to them.

An excellent patron saint for diocesan priests is Saint Phillip Neri. Basing himself at the parish Church of Saint Girolamo della Caritá, he did a marvelous work of spiritual direction and encouragement for both priests and lay people in 16th century Rome. One of his spiritual directors told him once he had no need to go to India to be a missionary since the city of Rome itself was his "India." As a priest he used to hear confessions from dawn to noon every day, and his cheerfulness and humility brightened the lives of thousands of people. The establishment of his oratory was a source of spiritual direction and authentic joy for many diocesan priests and has done great good for priests throughout the centuries. One famous example of this was the oratory established by Cardinal John Henry Newman for Catholic priests in England during the 19th century.

God's goodness is such that the more we help our brother priests, the more we are strengthened in our own vocation. They too will be praying for us and helping us, as is proper to the Communion of Saints. "The power of charity!" Saint Josemaria writes, "If you live that blessed brotherly spirit, your mutual weakness will also be a support to keep you upright in the fulfillment of duty—just as in a house of cards, one card supports the other." (*The Way* #462)

Another whole aspect of charity is speaking well of others. There has always been a friendly tradition of good-natured teasing among priests in the Church. Even our Lord teased His apostles, as when He nicknamed James and John the sons of thunder, or when He ironically rebuked his apostles about their sleepiness in the Garden of Gethsemane. A good sense of humor is always a delight in gatherings of priests, and helps to maintain a lively and happy atmosphere. But negative speech or gossip goes beyond good- natured teasing and friendship. Saint Columban, a sixth century Irish monk, once wrote, "Men like nothing better than discussing and minding the business of others, passing superfluous comments at random and criticizing people behind their backs." As priests striving to become saints we need to give good example to our brothers in priest gatherings. It's very easy and tempting to criticize others, especially certain priests or bishops. Besides being a sin against charity, such a carping attitude often demoralizes those who are listening. It can take away their hope and optimism for the Church, and lead to a useless kind of anger.

***

All of us see things from our own point of view, which may be quite incomplete or distorted. The adage is true: "if you cannot praise, say nothing." If that means that we have to change the conversation at times, so be it. If it means that we must be silent 50% of the time, so be it. Though it sounds a bit trite, silence is golden.

Of course there are times when we may speak of others' faults without committing the sin of detraction. We may have to speak with a certain person about a priest's problem, for the good of the priest himself and the Church. Or perhaps there is something that is truly bothering us about someone, and we can't find a solution. But these types of conversation should be done in a responsible way, with someone who can give good advice, and we will pray for the person in question. In certain cases our conversation about another may have to be with a superior in the diocese, as mentioned before. But we must not discuss the faults of others just to get a laugh, to appear clever or "in the know," or simply because everyone else is doing it. Many uncharitable remarks can also come from unresolved feelings of resentment and revenge towards a certain person; they are un-priestly and un-Christian, and we must promptly overcome with the help of God's grace.

It's a good and natural thing if we enjoy the company of some priests more than others. Part of this attraction may come from mutual interests or backgrounds, the fact that we are seminary classmates, or that we were ordained in the same year. It is indeed a pleasure and enjoyable break to spend our day off with a good priest friend or to go on a trip together. But we shouldn't be exclusive or cliquish in our friendship with priests. At social gatherings, let's try to take an interest in other priests as well. We needn't speak or sit with the same ones all the time. There may be priests with different interests, even different theological or liturgical approaches than ours—yet they are our brothers. Our own priesthood can be broadened and deepened by contact with others, even if they have different personalities and experiences than our own. Let's never forget that charity is the greatest and most beautiful virtue of all, and the first half of it is understanding. Once we understand someone, we can help him, which is the second half of charity.

As part of our fraternal spirit, we priests should also find time to pray together. Many priests form support groups which include a time for prayer, such as adoration before the Blessed Sacrament, or the praying of the Breviary. Such gatherings are also a perfect opportunity to exchange impressions and experiences with one another—hopefully without gossip or useless criticisms—and to have a common meal or other relaxing activity. As we see from the Gospels, the Lord Himself often found time to gather more intimately with His apostles and future priests, and told them many things, encouraging them both personally and as a group. We can be confident that when we gather with our brothers in the right spirit, with both fraternity and charity, Christ will be with us. We will be fulfilling to the letter what He Himself declared: "For where two or three are gathered in My name, there am I in the midst of them" (*Mt* 18:20).

There are two Hearts to whom we can always go to expand our understanding and fraternity with priests: the Sacred Heart of Jesus, who gave His apostles the new commandment of charity; and the Immaculate Heart of Mary, who loves each one of us because she sees in us the image of her Son. If we ever notice a distancing between ourselves and others, if bitterness or anger begins to grow in us—let's have immediate recourse to these two Hearts, who are so united and inter-connected. They will help us to forgive any offenses or mistrust that we might be experiencing, and with understanding to see the good works and virtues of our fellow priests. In many cases, we will discover that they are much better than we are.

MARY OUR MOTHER

Pope John Paul II once wrote: "Of the essence of motherhood is the fact that it concerns the person. Motherhood always establishes a unique and unrepeatable relationship between two people: *between mother and child, and child and mother*" (Encyclical Letter *Mother of the Redeemer*, 1987, p.63). Our personal relationship with the Blessed Virgin Mary began at our Baptism, in a most profound way. At that moment we became sons of God, members of the mystical body of Christ His Church, and sons of Mary. As the years go by, we want that relationship to deepen and become more tender, in much the same way as a good son loves his mother more deeply with every year that passes.

Though we're grown men, let's try to be as small children in dealing with Mary. In their first years children learn practically everything from their mothers, and we can do the same with the Blessed Mother. As priests we can particularly learn from her faith...that is, her belief in God's plan for her from the start. She said yes to her vocation in the most marvelous and eloquent way. Behold the handmaid, she declared, and God's grace entered into her completely. Shouldn't we respond in the same way as priests? The day of our ordination we were also called by name. The rest of our life is our response to that divine call. We need to open ourselves completely to the working of God's grace within us, as we pray, administer the sacraments, give spiritual guidance to our people, and help the poor. For us, Mary is a constant guide for faith and fidelity.

Imagine what reverence the Virgin of Nazareth would have with her Son, as she held Him and cared for Him as an infant. Perhaps she can help us to deal with Christ's Body and Blood in the same reverent way at Holy Mass and in administering Holy Communion. As we hold Him in our hands, as we distribute Him to the faithful, let's ask

His mother for reverence and piety always, even a certain tenderness which good mothers know how to give to the bodies of their children. *Mary, may I always treat your Son with the greatest delicacy and reverence, for His is the Body that saves the world...*

Pope John Paul II also speaks of her indomitable faith on Calvary. As her son is being killed before her eyes, she's experiencing the exact opposite of what the angel told her many years before: "He will be great...and the Lord God will give Him the throne of His father David, and He will reign over the house of Jacob for ever; and of His kingdom there will be no end" (*Lk* 1:32-33). And now, standing at the foot of the Cross, Mary is the witness, humanly speaking, of the complete *negation of those words*. On that wood of the Cross her Son hangs in agony as one condemned.....How great, how heroic then is the obedience of faith shown by Mary in the face of God's 'unsearchable judgments'!" (cf Encyclical Letter *Mother of the Redeemer*, n.18, 1987).

***

There may be times in our priesthood when we too can suffer true agony: scandals involving priests and bishops, including individuals we know; Catholics who blatantly dissent from the Church and who leave to join other religions; young people who turn from God to adopt immoral life-styles, despite all our teachings and warnings; a period of real darkness and even personal bitterness, for whatever cause, with very little consolation; the feeling of uselessness in our work. These are the moments, as little boys who feel lost, when we should have special recourse to Mary, Mother of Sorrows. Such moments are really a great privilege for us, since we are very close then to the sufferings of Mary and her Son; we can be true co-redeemers if we learn to cast our sorrows onto the fire of God's purifying love.

Mary's faith was greater than Abraham's since she believed that she could truly conceive a son without the intervention of a man. Her response in other words was completely supernatural. *Often times, Mary, when there is no human explanation for things; when a situation seems impossible, I will trust in you. Please ask God to send me the grace to persevere and to have hope in His Divine Power.*

But it is not only in the most trying or desperate moments that we should have recourse to Mary. We need her to teach us a faith that is not only "informative" but "performative"—to use the words of Benedict XVI in his second encyclical. We have performative or operative faith when we say our prayers on time each day, when we speak clearly about the moral teachings of the Church (all of them), when we exercise patience and kindness with those around us, when we finish a task that is unpleasant or boring. Perhaps in those moments we can ask Mary to be with us. We can accompany her in the ordinary tasks of her household so many years ago in Nazareth, when her entire life was taken up by the small chores of every day. We need to work in God's presence in much the same way as she did.

We should not expect applause or recognition for what we do. The only recognition that is worthwhile comes from Heaven; all other honors soon disappear and turn to dust. Our greatest honor should be to serve God and others as good priests. And here again we can learn from our Mother's faith. At Cana she was confident in her Son's power; she simply had to supply the occasion, to give Him a little motherly "push," so to speak. She is waiting to do the same for us, but she expects our faith and obedience to her son. For this reason, she will often tell us *Do whatever he tells you* (Jn 2:5). And she has every right to ask this of us, since that phrase also sums up her life of faith and obedience.

***

Mary then can never be only a doctrine of the Church for us, or simply a beautiful work of art—though such objects can inspire devotion in us. Above all, our relationship with her must be real and personal. We are not dealing with an object, or an artistic ideal—but a real woman who is now in Heaven and loves us deeply because we are priests of her son. We bring her son to the earth through the sacraments, especially the Holy Eucharist. We preach his word and bring people to his Church. What must be her love and favor for each one of us!

Let's learn to use our heart and human affections in dealing with Mary. "How does a normal son or daughter treat his mother? In different ways, of course, but never coldly. In an intimate way, through small, commonplace customs…..In our relationship with our mother in heaven, we should act in very much the same way" (St. Josemaría Escrivá, *Christ is Passing By*, n.142). We needn't be complicated in showing our love for her. Perhaps a simple greeting to her upon entering our room or office will do, taking advantage of a picture or statue of her. It's an excellent way to live in her presence. Aspirations also help, like "Hail full grace," "Refuge of sinners," "Cause of our joy." We can literally say hundreds of these while walking down the street, or driving. Or we can compose other ejaculations and short prayers of our own on certain occasions, such as on one of her feast days. If you have a poetic streak, you may even wish to dedicate a poem to her; she certainly is the most loveable inspiring woman who ever lived. We can be confident that in her hands our prayers and sacrifices will be used for the best result.

Many priests have made a personal consecration to her, often renewed in their lives. This can be very valuable for some, but you may wish simply to dedicate each day to her without the need for a formal consecration or vow. Certainly she will be most attentive to our needs when we go to her with humility and affection. I know of one priest who has a lovely laminated picture of Mary with her son on the dashboard of his car. It helps him to stay recollected when driving, as well as to prevent road rage, because he prays to her for all the drivers that he finds annoying.

So many priests throughout the centuries of course have found her to be their refuge and their strength in times of temptations against purity. The Memorare prayer can be most effective in those moments, since it is an invocation of such confidence and intensity. Remembering her virginity and complete dedication to God can be a powerful reminder to us in our own living of celibacy. She and her Son can send us the graces we need in the face of the strongest temptations. It's important to be calm and confident in those moments, knowing that with her behind us and watching over us, the evil one cannot harm us.

***

Called by Name

The same thing applies to any temptations we may have against faith or vocation. These are areas where the evil one will most try to attack us, especially as priests. Once we start doubting or questioning truths of Faith, or entertaining doubts of vocation, or harboring thoughts or desires against celibacy—Satan gains a clear advantage. Many of our brother priests over the centuries have been deceived by him, who at times can even appear as an "angel of light" under the guise of charity or devotion. But it is not true devotion or charity, but only an excuse for pride or lust. Let's call things by their names, and have quick recourse to Mary, like a small child who's being chased by a fierce dog. "Love our Lady," we read in *The Way*, "and she will obtain abundant grace to help you conquer in your daily struggle. And the enemy will gain nothing by those perversities that seem to boil up continually within you" (n. 493).

A devotion recommended by all the Popes is the recitation of the rosary. It is truly a loving wreath of roses that we place around her every time we say those decades with affection. "Hail full of grace, the Lord is with thee…Blessed are you among women" (*Lk*: 1.28.42). Those greetings were the joyful salutations of her vocation, when the angel Gabriel announced God's eternal plan of love to her, and when her cousin Elizabeth recognized her unique honor among all women. By repeating those words, again and again, we are giving her special veneration as well as joy. At times our minds might be distracted during the rosary, but this should not be a motive for giving up this centuries-old devotion, recommended not only by the Popes but also by our Lady herself in her various apparitions approved by the Church. In saying the rosary we should remember that our intention is to please not ourselves, but her. If a young man in serenading his sweetheart gets distracted for a minute, he still keeps singing his song, and the young woman is cherishing every word that she hears. Shouldn't we be the same with Mary when we say the rosary, and teach others to have the same attitude?

The Rosary is also a great contemplative prayer, a simple way of entering more and more into the lives of Mary and her Son. "Against the background of the words Ave Maria, the principal events of the life of Jesus Christ pass before the eyes of the soul. They take shape in the complete series of the joyful, sorrowful and glorious mysteries, and they put us in living communion with Jesus through—we might say—the heart of his Mother" (Pope John Paul II, Apostolic Letter *On the Most Holy Rosary*, n.2). By saying the rosary in a contemplative way, little by little we will find our own lives transformed into theirs. We will be with Joseph adoring the child in Bethlehem, we shall be with Mary at the crucifixion, we shall rejoice with all of Heaven at her Assumption. And now, with the Mysteries of Light, we can be with Christ and His mother at the key events of His public ministry, including the miracle of Cana. A contemplative saying of the rosary thus elevates our thoughts and our life onto a higher plane. It can also unite us more closely with our brother priests, as we pray for those particularly in need.

At the end of his Apostolic Letter Pope John Paul II speaks about the family rosary, but it can easily be applied to our brother priests who also say the rosary: "*The family that prays together stays together. The Holy Rosary, by age-old tradition, has shown itself particularly effective as a prayer which brings the family together. Individual family members, in turning their eyes toward Jesus, also regain the ability to look one another in the eye, to communicate, to show solidarity, to forgive one another and to see their covenant of love renewed in the Spirit of God*" (Pope John Paul II, *On the Most Holy Rosary*, n.41). If such good things can happen to members of a blood-related family, they can also happen to us priests when we pray with our brothers in the priesthood.

***

Small children are always asking their mother for things, to the point of becoming annoying. We should have no such fear with Mary. Let's keep in mind that she is the daughter of God the Father, the Mother of God the Son, and the Spouse of God the Holy Spirit. She is in the best position to listen to our pleas, and to grant us what we need. Through her humility she crushes the devil's head, who is a cause of so many crimes and disasters in this world. But Mary knows how to protect us from him, and desires to help us in all of our needs—both big and small. What is it that you hold most dear to your heart, Father?

I know one priest who said three Hail Marys while he was hunting, and immediately a splendid wild turkey appeared in the sights of his gun. You may have a few similar requests at times, and even greater more serious ones.

Let's keep asking our Lady of Guadalupe for the protection of innocent human life worldwide, especially the lives of the unborn at all stages from conception to birth. They are the smallest and most defenseless beings of the entire human family, and we beg the Mother of God to end the plague of violence against them. We certainly pray for more vocations to the Church, for those in the religious life, for priests, for dedicated lay faithful who can serve Christ in the middle of society. We ask her for the poor and the unemployed, and for their families—as we do all that we can to stir up people's awareness and consciences on the need to assist them. We pray for world peace, especially for an end to terrorism and the root causes behind it. There are so many intentions we could add: the strengthening and protection of the authentic family as the union between a man and a woman, the cleansing of the entertainment industry, the conversion of others to the one Church founded by Christ, with the fullness of truth. Yes we can even pray to her, especially Our Lady of Fatima, for the great miracle of the conversion of the Muslims. Though they now outnumber Catholics as the largest religion in the world, Mary's power shall not be lacking. She is, in the words of Saint Thomas Aquinas, "Omnipotentia Suplicans," all powerful in her petition.

Hail Mary Mother of God, pray for us!

Made in the USA
Charleston, SC
09 March 2012